A CUP OF COMFORT®

for

MILITARY FAMILIES

Stories that celebrate
heroism on the
home front

Edited by Colleen Sell

Avon, Massac

D0818280

In loving memory of my grandfather, Frank Joseph Baum

A *Cup of Comfort*® is a registered trademark of F+W Publications, Inc.

Published by
Adams Media, an F+W Publications Company
57 Littlefield Street, Avon, MA 02322 U.S.A.
www.adamsmedia.com and *www.cupofcomfort.com*

ISBN-10: 1-59869-864-8
ISBN-13: 978-1-59869-864-0

Printed in the United States of America.

J I H G F E D C B A

Library of Congress Cataloging-in-Publication Data
is available from the publisher.

This publication is designed to provide accurate and authoritative information with regard to the subject matter covered. It is sold with the
understanding that the publisher is not engaged in rendering legal,
accounting, or other professional advice. If legal advice or other expert
assistance is required, the services of a competent professional person
should be sought.

—From a *Declaration of Principles* jointly adopted by
a Committee of the American Bar Association and
a Committee of Publishers and Associations

Many of the designations used by manufacturers and sellers to distin-
guish their products are claimed as trademarks. Where those designations appear in this book and Adams Media was aware of a trademark
claim, the designations have been printed with initial capital letters.

This book is available at quantity discounts for bulk purchases.
For information, please call 1-800-289-0963.

Contents

Acknowledgments

I am most thankful to the writers who have shared their personal stories in this book. Writing is always an act of courage; writing deeply personal stories about the impact of military life on those who serve in the military and their loved ones takes extraordinary courage and grace.

As always, Adams Media provided me with an army of able and willing support—most notably Meredith O'Hayre (my captain), Paula Munier (my colonel), Laura Daly, Jacquinn Williams, and Virginia Beck.

My deepest love, respect, and gratitude go to the soldiers who have most influenced and inspired my life—my father, Albert Sell, and my late grandfather, Frank Baum.

May God bless and keep all the men and women in the armed forces and their loved ones.

Introduction

*"The strength of a nation derives from
the integrity of the home."*

—*Confucius*

I was not raised in a military family, nor did I raise
my children in a military family. But the residual
effects of my father's and my grandfather's military
service definitely had an impact on all our lives.

By the time I was on the way, my father had
completed his stint in the Army. Though Dad broke
his nose and shattered an eardrum during his tour of
duty in Germany, our country was not at war, and
his injuries were not combat-related. That did not
make it any less difficult for my parents to be apart
for the pregnancy and birth of their first child and
during the first six months of her life. I've often wondered if my sister felt his absence.

I also suspect that my dad's fastidiousness is due, in part, to his military training. That definitely carried over to his parenting: shoes lined up, beds crisply made, posture straight. Surely, the telling and retelling of the story of how Dad broke his nose (compliments of an officer he'd told where to put his command not to go call my pregnant mother) both amused and influenced his six kids. It told us that even a gentle man like my father must sometimes fight for what's right. Other than that, my dad's military experience had no impact on our family.

But my grandfather's did.

Frank Joseph Baum eloped with my maternal grandmother when I was a toddler. They'd met six years earlier at the U.S. Army War College in Carlisle, Pennsylvania. Grandma dated the tall, lanky soldier from Brooklyn for a while, but then he went to Korea and she moved with family to Ohio. Then one day, he showed up on our doorstep. He and Grandma went on a date . . . and three days later came back married. I love that story as much as I love the one about Dad's broken nose.

And I loved Grandpa's stories. He had a million of them, all filled with wisdom and humor. Some were of the M*A*S*H–like antics of his Army buddies. As an adult, I came to realize that many of his entertaining, lesson-filled stories were shaped by his military experience. His stories informed, inspired, and guided my life and my siblings' lives—and by extension, our children's and grandchildren's lives.

I was even more affected, though, by the stories Grandpa didn't tell. He never spoke to us of his war experiences in the Philippines and Korea or of "cleaning up" after the atomic bombs in Japan. He never told us about being the driver of a tank in which every other soldier onboard was killed, including his best buddy, whose head was blown off. My parents finally told us that story when we were old enough to understand the answer to the question we'd asked for years, "Why doesn't Grandpa drive?" But those stories, those nightmarish experiences, were always there, festering inside my grandfather, dulled only by the alcoholism that nearly killed him before he finally, when I was in my teens, defeated that enemy. Though Grandpa never shared the memories that haunted him, somehow we knew he'd been through hell and back, many times. Those stories were written on his soul.

We also knew he'd made tremendous sacrifices and done an honorable and courageous thing, because our parents did tell us the stories of how Grandpa had left his "big-shot" Manhattan banking career to join the effort to defeat Hitler. How his wife had divorced him while he was on the front lines overseas. How he had earned medals for his outstanding service to our country. How, upon his return, he was not allowed to see his two sons—ever again—but continued to provide for them. Grandpa never got over that loss, but I hope that being a beloved member of our family helped to ease his pain. I'm sorry, for their sake, that his sons did not know their father. He was a brilliant, compassionate, and noble man. And a wonderful stepfather, grandfather, and great-grandfather to those privileged to know him before his death in 1989—in part from the effects of radiation exposure.

Only after my grandmother's death did we see a glimpse of what Grandpa had seen. That's when my mother found the photographs he'd taken of war and its aftermath. That's when she found the many medals he'd earned. That's when we really understood why he could not share those stories. A kind and conscientious man, Grandpa would not have burdened us with those horrific memories. A humble man, he would not have worn his medals on his chest. Instead, he gave us a lifetime of wise and joyful stories to pass along to our children and grandchildren.

I hope the insightful and inspiring stories in this book, written by military families encompassing several eras and all branches of the armed forces, bring you the same comfort that my grandfather's stories, and life, brought to me.

—Colleen Sell

The Illusion

I write this sitting on my bed in my room, a room much like a dorm room in a college or barracks. My laptop computer sits on a small wooden table that another airman here before me made and eventually discarded behind the pods, as we military types call them, the trailer-like living quarters I live in. I found this little table there one night as I scavenged for exactly those sorts of things, cleaned it up and made it mine, a small comfort that makes this place a bit more like home.

In my room are two steel bunk beds with two mattresses, worn and beaten down. I have my own pillow, sheets, and comforter that I brought from home, an amenity that keeps me from those itchy wool blankets the military seems to love so much. There are also two wooden wardrobes, each with a mirror inside and a closet rod. The walls are light wood paneling and the floors an off-white linoleum tile.

This room is quite civilized and comfortable compared to the tents I've lived in before. Of course, there are pros and cons to both styles of living, but you'd have to have experienced them both to really understand. The wall air conditioner is kept as cold as it goes. Its gentle humming is a nice source of white noise to drown out all of the other noises around. My roommate and I place dryer sheets over the air conditioner's intake to filter the air, a trick that gives the room a nice, clean smell. It lasts for about a week before they are so dirty they fall off from the weight of the dust they've collected. Sometimes when I watch movies on my laptop, my mini/mobile entertainment center, I eventually get so cold that I have to get under the sheets, but I never turn down the AC for fear that I'll forget to turn it back up and wake up in a pool of sweat, a lesson learned from prior experience.

I have a small coffee maker. I brew German coffee that I buy here at the BX/PX and sometimes some pecan-torte–flavored coffee that my wife sends me in her loving care packages. It fills the room with a wonderful, sweet aroma that makes me feel relaxed and at home.

Eventually, all of the coffee drinking and cold air brings about that old familiar call of nature. So I get up from the bed, my only chair, and slip on my shoes, tuck my shirt into my gym shorts, and get myself back into regulation dress, even in physical training

(PT) gear. I smooth the comforter back into place so that the sheets don't get cold and bugs can't get in, and I open up my door. Usually I'm surprised by the light of the day. I work at night, so I don't see daylight very often and when I do it's unpleasant at first. But working at night is a great way to do business. The biggest perk is that the temperature drops down to the 80s and 90s, down 30 degrees from the 120s during the day. Working at night also gives you the advantage of not being easily seen. I operate cargo aircraft, and being big and slow isn't the best defense against all of the people here who would like to show a video of shooting me down . . . but I digress.

After my eyes have had a second to adjust to the daylight, the cozy smell of my clean aromatic room is replaced with the smell of burning tires and waste. Dust rushes in to fill my nostrils. This lovely aroma stems from the thin dusty air and the "burn pit" that this base uses to dispose of all of the large trash in the country—a medical hazard to say the least, but effective for getting rid of unwanted tires and feces along with any other trash that can be burnt and reduced. The cold air that chilled my skin is replaced with the dry oven-like heat of the desert. This country is so old, the land so rich with history, that even the desert sand has turned to dust. The locals learned to dress in robes and to cover their faces millennia ago. It's not so much cultural or religious as it is survival instincts kicking in. The hot, dry air swirls around your face, stinging your eyes. Everyone here wears glasses, and most of the Americans wear ballistic goggles made to look cool, like Oakleys. The fact that we don't wear head dressings or face masks leaves us with a chalky taste in our mouths at all times. The dust reaches into every crevice; there is nothing clean here, only the attempt at cleanliness.

Before I left home, on my last day in the United States, I waited in a hotel to get on a plane to fly twenty-six hours to my first stop in the area of responsibility (AOR), the geographic area of the war. As I got out of the shower and got dressed into my desert camouflage uniform (DCUs), I thought to myself, *This is the last time I'm truly going to be clean for the next four months.* We all carry hand sanitizer and wash before we do anything in an attempt to keep from spreading more germs, but after a while it all seems a bit futile. But we all do it. It's a wonderful illusion, just like my room—a dorm room at some college, not a pod in Iraq. The illusion is broken every time a helicopter flies overhead at 100 feet or a fighter aircraft takes off in full after-burner. Every time the all-too-familiar thud of a mortar round hits close by and the following "alarm reds," "incoming," or "all clear" mantras are announced over the "giant voice" system. Sometimes the faint sounds of gunfire let everyone know it'll be a busy night in the base ICU.

The realities of base life in Iraq break the illusion for a few moments, but the longer you're here, the shorter the break. This is what my days "off" are like: I wake up, get some chow, go to the gym, and go back to my pod to experience the illusion until it is time to go to sleep. Tomorrow I fly, and in the air there is no time for illusion. There is no time for my beloved family. There is no time for faithful friends. No time for anything but the aircraft and the world I am flying in. As a navigator, I tell the pilots where to go and how to get there without hitting "no fly" areas or thunderstorms. I keep us out of the controllable parts of harm's way. I also watch for and direct evasive action for missile fire, small arms fire, and anti-aircraft artillery fire from the ground. This is an unfortunate part of the job that I have had to employ more times than I would've liked and many more times than I'll ever be able tell my wife.

Oddly, the nature of my business is both dangerous and beautiful. I've seen the sunset over Mosul with red-orange glows gently caressing the silhouettes of tall palm trees and domed mosques. I've seen some of Saddam Hussein's palaces in Baghdad that are as ornate and giant as castles in any storybook. My eyes have been privy to so many sights that only another warrior, or perhaps a poet, would truly appreciate. You get one second, one small fraction of a moment, to enjoy the spectacle, and then it's gone. The sunset in Mosul, so gorgeous and serene, I barely had time to snap a quick picture before a missile warning indication echoed through the aircraft. I saw the palaces in Baghdad framed against a sea of houses that makes up Sadr City illuminated by the fierce and bright glow of an explosion, and the reactive flares shot out from the convoy under attack. This is the reality that is Iraq: dangerous and beautiful.

Now that I've described the illusion that aids me in a moment's relaxation and peace of mind during a stressful time, please do not mistake the illusion as a mental block of reality from a state of some dementia and inability to deal with the real world. Rather, the illusion is a simple automatic daydream. It's what one might call complacency in a low-threat environment. It is the same illusion we all use while driving home from work, traveling a route so familiar that you can allow your mind to drift away to some other place and still be functioning at the wheel. The difference is that, here, it is a mortar round landing within earshot that wakens me, while at home it is the brake lights of the vehicle in front of me.

This difference is that my reality, when it comes back, stays a bit longer, because I have to transition from this reality back to "normal." The mind can get confused. Most get used to the mortars, the giant voice, the fighter aircraft, and helicopter sounds. The silence at home can actually be deafening when you lie down and no longer hear the humming of the air conditioner drowning out the sounds of war.

Things could be much worse. I have it quite nice compared to many, because I have relative safety, enough to have my illusion. I have my pod, my air conditioning, and my little wooden table. I have the pictures that my two-year-old daughter finger-painted hung up on my wooden wardrobe. I have photos of my wife and daughter and the sonograms of my other daughter "on the way" that I look at nightly on the top bunk of my bed. Mostly, I have the reality of good friends and a strong family that I have at home waiting for me.

The illusion is the small bit of reality lost for a short time. Home, where my loved ones are, there are no mortars, bullets, fighters, helos, or all of the things that make Iraq, well, Iraq. But for now, I am here. So I sit here writing this on my laptop, sitting on my bed in my dorm room, safe and sound as a fighter aircraft takes off, muffled by the drone of the air conditioning.

—*Justin R. Ballard*

Cry for Happy

A sodden blanket of summer air lay over the bay. Even the birds sought refuge in the thick scrub oaks hovering above the cluster of forlorn house trailers. My mother stared into this sweltering corner of Panama City, Florida, face moist and shining, wishing out loud to be anywhere else. And I watched the sky as jets passed overhead, wondering why I had to be torn from my high school the year before I graduated. I think we both wanted to connect, just for a moment, to those we once knew.

"This humidity is killing me," my mother said. "I wish we were back at Kingsley Field in Klamath Falls." My stepfather, my sister, and I all wished it too.

But my mom, after four years at the out-of-the-way Air Force base in Klamath Falls, Oregon, had yearned to be down South again, nearer her relatives in Georgia. So my stepfather applied for, and got, a transfer to Tyndall Air Force Base, just across the bay from where we were now sweating.

"Even Victorville. Oh, to be back in the dry heat of the desert in Victorville," she said to no one in particular. "Hot summers, but boy we never did sweat like this." Her subdued Southern accent flared like the heat waves writhing off the tops of the house trailers.

Our military transience began when I was only five years old. That's when my mother remarried. She left me with my aunt in Fairburn, Georgia, a small town just south of Atlanta, and flew out to Hollywood to visit her sister, who was chasing uniforms at the time and must have told my mom that there were plenty to go around. My mom quickly found an Air Force staff sergeant. Soon after, she flew home to pack me and our bags, and the next thing I knew we were waving goodbye to my beloved Aunt Pat as she stood in the driveway by the well house, tears running down her cheeks. I knew only that we were going somewhere. And my Aunt Pat was not coming with us.

Nearing the end of the last in a series of airplane rides, I pressed my nose to the cold window and reveled in the glorious sight of the lights of Los Angeles below us. I was half asleep as a strange man carried me to a car and drove us to a motel in a town in the desert. The next day we drove to George Air Force Base near Victorville, California, and a housing area of pastel stucco dwellings, six units joined like train cars in a tight U-turn. These arrangements filled both sides of the street and seemed to cover the earth.

Families surrounded us. Kids of all ages rode bikes, pulled wagons, and roller-skated up and down the sidewalks of the housing area. Women carried baskets of laundry to the community washing machines and outdoor clotheslines that butted against the long row of car stalls that serviced the six-unit housing modules. Friendships flared like gas fires, and before I knew it I was playing games in the gritty brown dirt and tumbleweeds near the clotheslines. Kids in the housing units found playmates and bonded quickly, and before too long, I felt at home.

Far from the closeness and attention of Georgia relatives, far from those who knew and loved her, Mom cried often as she busied herself making a new home in the California desert.

Then Iris Richardson, fresh from Little Rock, Arkansas, appeared one hot day from the unit next door, carrying a wicker basketful of wash. Mom stepped out the door at the same time with her own basket. For the next six years, both women conducted a Southern-accent duet as if joined since birth. Their friendship cemented quickly, and I think my mother's love of the desert began when she and Iris first met on that hot laundry day.

As I sat playing in the brown dust and tumbleweeds with my new friends, it was good to see my mother talking and laughing while hanging clothes in the desert heat with her new friend.

Iris and her husband, Alden, an Air Force sergeant like my new dad, acted as the first catalyst of the molecular attraction that gathered military families into tight-knit units when packed into the subdivisions with obscure names such as "Wherry" and "Capehart." Wherry and Capehart, senators from Nebraska and Indiana, respectively, gladly offered their names in 1949 to the new military housing areas that provided fertile grounds for friendships to develop.

But friendships of this kind were quickly severed with a transfer to another military base. Threads of transferred families might then cross again in some other location, like the weavings of a tapestry, in and out of the units appropriated by Senators Wherry and Capehart. But I made friends quickly and had no knowledge of the fleeting nature of those new relationships. And six years with my new dad took on a permanency that felt okay. As I grew in those six years in Victorville, so did the bond between Iris and Mom.

Outside by the bakery truck or the ice cream truck, conversation branched in any number of directions, most commonly upcoming bingo night at the enlisted men's club on Wednesdays. And if I was lucky, Mom would take me along. I don't know which I enjoyed most, the excitement of the bingo games and the possibility of winning something or the labyrinthine web of conversation and laughter that constantly punctuated the evening. The more Mom and Iris laughed, the more Shirley Temples and French fries I got to consume.

But six years at the same base was almost unheard of in the military, and in the spring of 1958, word arrived that my dad's squadron had been transferred to Thule, Greenland. Since families could not go to Greenland, we would spend the next year near our relatives, including my Aunt Pat, in Fairburn, Georgia. The military packs and leaves quickly, and the next thing we knew Iris was a tiny waving person growing smaller and smaller through the car's rear window.

Even though the week-long drive to Georgia held the reality for my mom of "going home," it also carried with it the deep wound of separation, and as the Burma Shave signs slipped by on Route 66, she cried often while speaking of Iris and Alden. We had just experienced our first of several uprootings.

I'm not sure I knew what to think as I stared at the desert slipping by, heat waves blurring the distant mountains. I had spent the first six years of school at the same location, where I had waved to many of my friends as they left for other bases. And now I was the one leaving. It felt odd, and I sensed a faint emptiness. Although we were returning to Georgia to be near relatives, as far as I was concerned I had no school and no friends. I felt snatched from my soil—exposed.

The year in Georgia without my dad seemed long and lonely. Although we were near aunts, uncles, and cousins, there was still the task of making new friends. Mother's frenetic correspondence with Iris kept the coals alive, even when Alden and Iris were transferred to Germany. But the cloud of knowing that our stay in Georgia was only for a year cast its shadow over me. Although I knew my classmates, I developed few new bonds and found myself seeking the companionship of my cousin whenever possible. Short of that, I rode my bike and roamed the woods alone.

The year passed. Dad came home, and belongings were boxed for the quick move to Klamath Falls, Oregon, just three weeks prior to my completion of seventh grade. The feeling of being a transient among "civilians" and a couple of fistfights with local boys had planted ambivalence in me, and my only regret was leaving my Aunt Pat and cousins. I was ready to leave, yet apprehensive about starting the process again.

The fresh family roots were ripped up again and replanted in the isolated housing area in the Klamath Basin, five miles from the air base, surrounded by sagebrush, irrigation canals, and potato fields. The contacts with former friends unraveled a bit more, yet the connection with Iris remained a lifeline for Mom, as she pressed what tender roots remained into the rocky soil of Oregon.

Among many other Air Force brats, I made new friendships easily. The common bond of many "wing nuts" provided protection from the "potato-herder" farm kids at the local high school to which we were bussed.

Then came the unspeakable. After three years, Alden and Iris transferred out of Germany and the connection broke. The letters ceased. Perhaps in the mad shuffle of moving and packing, addresses and phone numbers were lost or family problems arose or . . . my mother hesitated to think what could be the matter. For the first time in ten years, she had no way of contacting Iris and wondered out loud why Iris did not contact her. In retrospect, that may have been one of the reasons that Mom developed a dislike for Klamath Falls, yearned to be near her relatives, and pushed Dad for a transfer.

So there we were. Friendless again. Sweating in the subtropical Gulf Coast summer. Finding it difficult to breathe, much less settle into a new community, make new friends, and establish new roots. We stood there, just three days into our temporary stay in the dripping, dismal trailer park, waiting our turn to move into Capehart housing on the base.

There are times when the fabric of life seems torn and frayed. Lost is its definition of warp and woof and any connection to the pattern that once seemed so clear. This hot, heavy, sweating place was just such a time. So we stood, the trailer next to us only about fifteen feet away, compressing the stagnant air between us.

"Rachel?" The trailer spoke. From a small-screened window high on the green, moss-tinted wall, a high-pitched voice called. "Rachel Wilbourn?"

Mom turned to the tiny window, trying to make sense of the voice, squinting to see a face.

"Rachel Wilbourn?" The pitch of the voice rose and, with it, an air of anxiety. "Is that you?" The voice bore an unmistakable Southern accent.

Mom stepped quickly toward the window, mouth open so that I could almost see the quickness of her breath.

Then, "Well, I'll Swanee! It *is* you, Rachel!"

Mom could not contain herself. "Iris? Iris? Is that you, Iris?" She almost clawed at the screen as the two women sputtered.

"Rachel!"

"Iris!"

"Oh, Rachel!"

"Iris, Iris, I can't believe this!"

The trailer rocked as Iris bounded out the door on the opposite side. She sprinted around the end, and Mom plunged into her outstretched arms in an embrace that formed a single, Southern, sobbing mass. Eventually, my sister and I got in our hugs amidst trails of happy tears as Alden emerged from a sweating nap to wrap his ample arms around us all.

The unbelievable coincidence of it all so overwhelmed us that it hurt to speak so fast, to cry and to breathe at the same time. All the while, as I looked at my mother hopelessly wiping the tears that would not stop, I could see the loneliness, the separation, and the interminable ache of not knowing seep into the sand at her feet along with her tears. Cry for happy—as the Japanese so simply state—cry for happy and your tears comfort you.

And even though I was older, facing my last year of high school, friendless and apprehensive, things now seemed somehow better. Something had been reconnected. I could see that the wanderings of little threads had crossed again.

That day, forty-five years ago, cemented the relationship between my mom and Iris, which has since weathered everything the military, retirement, and aging have thrown at it.

—Terence M. Shumaker

Miracle at Sea

This has to be a dream, I thought, though I had been awake for more than an hour. I stood on the deck of the transporter ship and watched as the sun lifted from the sea. As word had it, the Navy was zigzagging our Army troops across the Pacific to Washington, after which I'd head east to Indiana to receive my discharge papers. Supposedly, the war was over. Around me, the clamor of rousing soldiers talking about their hopes of what they'd find and do upon returning home drifted on the wind.

Two and half years had passed since I'd seen any member of my family. The anticipation of being with them again was so great I could concentrate on nothing else as the shifting sea slapped against the ship. At age twenty-one, I had left home and joined the Army, ignoring the exemption I had been offered due to my enrollment in college. I set out to serve my country with the pride and the respect for responsibility with which I'd been raised.

Lulled by the rhythm of the sea and the thought of home so near, my mind drifted back to when Dad cut hair and when each of us boys—six of us—staked our claim in the business world by shining shoes. I loved it, crouched on the sidewalk outside Dad's barbershop door, interacting with people. Dad loved it, too. He also loved music. We used to joke that if he didn't stop tapping his feet in church, we would have to switch pews, because he was wearing the carpet thin. When my brothers and I sang, Dad would come up and stand really close so he could immerse himself in the harmony. What I wouldn't have given to be singing with my brothers right now.

Thirty months was a long time to be gone, and I was anxious to get back. Although we'd been told we were going home, allied warships roamed the area and a sailor stood watch. No word was final until your feet hit the soil. Sometimes, all a man could rely on were his memories . . . and hope. Hope carried me through each day and helped me to look forward to the next.

My next glance out over the water took in a tiny blue speck in the distance. I squinted for a better look: a warship, one of many we'd seen these past few days, but there was a familiarity about this one.

Mom and Dad's letters had described my brother's ship in detail. They always included nuggets of Jim's letters that instructed: "Tell John . . ." "Ask him if he saw . . ." "Make sure he . . ." The letters kept me close to home and all of us battling and working together toward a common goal. My heart swelled with emotion over the memories Jim and I shared, and I knew he was out there somewhere. But what were the odds that my brother's sub chaser would be in such close proximity? Still, I had to know. I had memorized the number on the side of the ship for this reason. If he were close, I wanted him to know I saw him.

I located a pair of binoculars and watched until I could make out the letters on the bow: SC 994. No! I looked again. Black letters over blue: SC 994. It was Jim's ship! Too shocked to care about protocol, I flew past the sailor standing guard at the gate that led to the fly bridge and ran up the stairs to the sailor on watch.

"Is there any way you can signal that sub chaser?" I pointed in the distance, trembling at the thought of being so near to one of my family. "I think my brother is on that ship. I want him to know I'm here, right here!"

Even if we weren't able to see or talk to each other for the duration of the war, just knowing we were so close would fill the hole of homesickness that had been chiseled out of my heart these past couple of years. I hoped it would do the same for Jim.

The sailor grinned, whether at my shaking or the odds of such a miracle, I didn't know, but he swung the light around so the sub chaser could see the coded signal.

"The angle's not right; I'm not sure he can see it." The sailor tried again, but there was no response from the chaser. He moved the light and tried again to signal out the message. It was taking too long; the chaser would be gone.

I had been injured in battle three times, but no physical pain hurt more than knowing how near I'd come to making contact with my brother only to fail. I left the bridge heavy-hearted and wandered back onto the deck to share with the guys what had happened. They understood my disappointment, the need to affirm family, a life, and a tie to something more than a cause so great it's easy to feel lost in it. Then I remembered that these guys were my brothers, too—my surrogate family. I was grateful for the friendships and bonds we'd developed, and some of the guys didn't have family to ponder over. So I dropped the matter and went about my day.

"Hey, private, you're wanted by the captain."

I roused myself off the deck and followed the sailor to where the captain stood surveying the horizon. By now, the sun was high in the sky, but a nice breeze kept the air cool and refreshing.

"Private, I understand your brother is on the *USS SC 994*. They came within view, but we were unsuccessful in contacting them."

"Yes, sir."

"Of all men . . . you, with your positive thoughts, staying faith, and commitment." It appeared he had some difficulty holding back a smile. I couldn't imagine where this was headed. I had broken protocol by approaching the bridge without permission, but it was an unusual circumstance and hadn't caused a problem. I didn't understand why he wanted to see me. "I think you probably deserve this more than anyone."

"Deserve what, sir?"

"We weren't able to signal the sub chaser your brother was on, but the message was intercepted by another ship in the area." He broke out into a full grin. "Your brother knows you're here. He knows you saw him."

Time closed in on that moment. The ship stopped, the clouds paused, and I was home. Laughs rang around a dining-room table, songs drifted on a summer evening breeze, and home felt as real as if I were standing in the middle of the family room talking with Dad.

"Thank you, sir."

Cheers erupted across the ship as word spread of this miracle at sea.

In the middle of the Pacific Ocean, the crew from Jim's sub chaser tied up next to our transporter. While sailors and soldiers bartered for goods plundered in Okinawa, my brother and I sat on the deck and talked for an entire afternoon.

That memory remains etched in my mind and continues to carry me through times when I feel uncertain. It affirms that miracles do happen, if for no other reason than to bring joy and hope to those who need it and to those who are willing to embrace it.

—*Tammera Ayers, as told by Reverend John Wine*

Respectful Warrior

In the darkness of his dreams, he stood on the heaving deck of the surfaced submarine. The crippled enemy vessel was so close he could hear it groan as seawater rushed into the holes torn in the hull by torpedoes. Pressed down by tons of water to its final moorage on the ocean floor, the stricken vessel became a tomb for the men trapped inside.

But I never knew it, not until long after my dad's death.

In my world, Dad wore the workaday olive of Air Force fatigues—it's what he wore into the maternity ward at Elmendorf Air Force Base in the Territory of Alaska when I was born in 1957.

He worked in offices or in the motor pool or driving a school bus so the kids on base could go to a Catholic school. His jobs kept changing, and I never questioned it. I was little, and for me, if there was snow on the ground in Alaska or fireflies in the air in North Carolina, life was as it should be.

Eventually, the man who lived next door always went by the name of "numb nuts," and it seemed hard for Dad to get along. I figured other people must be difficult, not my dad, because he always rescued animals who were lost or hurting. Even with us, he wasn't always comfortable in his own skin, but his gentle heart showed. I remember him weeping with me when our dog was hit by a car. One year he bought my mom a dozen birthday cards because he loved her so much, and each one captured his feelings just right—and then he couldn't decide how to sign any of them. He hand-carved a wooden biplane for me and painted it sage green, a color I still love.

Now, as an adult, I remember the nervous breakdown. Every day while Dad was "away," Mom and I would go for a doughnut and a Coca-Cola after school.

Dad came back with stories about a man who wanted to shave off his eyebrows, but somehow Dad's soul didn't come back with him.

Now, the memories come, unbidden. It happens when an unseen breeze ripples an American flag or when a bugler plays the haunting litany of taps. And always when I see veterans, I see my father again.

I remember him sitting in his familiar recliner, staring into the distance beyond the living room window. Years after his death, I finally understood that sometimes he wasn't looking at the world outside; he was looking within, at memories of times long past.

He shared the good memories. He kept the haunting ones to himself, enduring them alone.

My father was nervous, unable to sit still for long. Instead, his foot tapped, his knees wiggled, his fingers drummed. I was too much like him. His nervousness tore at me, sparked my own restlessness, and I didn't like it. As a teen I hid in my room. Looking back, I expect my dad envied me that luxury.

When hormonal storms and the illusion that I knew more than my parents took hold, I forgot the man who rushed home from a hard day to play the harmonica for his baby girl, to dance with me, and to rock me to sleep—if he didn't fall asleep first. My mind erased the tracks he left in the snow, trudging through sub-zero weather in Anchorage to buy me a wagon small enough to pull through our tiny home. I forgot the man who bent over and pushed me through the short hallways in a shoebox when I snubbed the shiny new wagon. I never knew how sore it made his back until Mom told me.

Later, when adolescence was no longer an excuse, I forgot to make things right between us. Oh, there was nothing obviously wrong between us. But Dad worried so much and always feared the worst, so I kept my distance, always at the shallow end of the relationship—except when a brutal diagnosis crowded out the invisible barriers.

When reality took a hammer to me, I dropped my guard and critical attitude long enough to fall into his strong, loving arms. The doctor's call came on my nineteenth birthday, when I first heard my name used in a sentence along with the words "cancer surgery" and "malignant melanoma." Mom consoled me through the day, and later that evening, when I gave in to the tears, my weary head came to rest against my father's chest. I heard the steady heartbeat of the man who'd helped give me life, and I wept through my fears, safe in the embrace of a man who would've surely given his life for me. His anxieties had often pushed me away, but this time they had saved my life; he had insisted I see the doctor.

I kept waiting for Dad to change his nervous, overprotective ways, to stop expecting the worst from people and life. And while I waited, our visits remained uneasy, difficult. I never paused to consider that he might not have been that way by choice.

I didn't know, because I wasn't there when his sensitive nature was scarred. On one solitary day in his span of years, his idealism faced off with a harsh reality that sent it running away, screaming. I saw the aftermath, the ugliness of the wound. I didn't know him well enough as an adult, and I never got to meet the man he was before the world wore him down.

My dad enlisted in the Navy during World War II, and charged into the fray as a naïve youth of eighteen. The momentum carried him through twenty years of honorable service to his country.

I heard—over and over—the stories of his adventures in Australia. But not until after his death did I hear the story of a battle on a different sea. He buried the details beyond telling, in a dark, desolate corner of his soul, beyond anyone's reach. My mother learned the truth after his death, in a letter from his youngest sister.

The letter explained the scar that outlived the war. Dreams dragged him back to the horror, night after night. Waking in tears and to the sound of his own screams, he'd wash down another sedative and try to forget. But again and again, his subconscious carried him back to those troubled waters, where he relived the brutal memory.

In the darkness of his dreams, he stood on the heaving deck of the surfaced submarine. He could hear the crippled enemy vessel groan. Seawater rushed into the holes torn in the hull by torpedoes. Pressed down by tons of water to its final moorage on the ocean floor, the stricken vessel became a tomb for the men trapped inside.

Those who escaped the sinking hulk thrashed in the frigid waters. Bubbles rose from below as every bit of air was pressed out of the collapsing hull. As each bubble burst, so did any hope that those sailors might see home again.

And then, even the water was on fire, as spilled fuel from the sunken vessel ignited. In a sea awash with faces, each wave crested with a cry for help in its wake. All that was right and fair and good demanded that they be taken prisoners of war. That didn't happen.

The captain ". . . surfaced and churned among the poor men who were dying and drowning and burning . . ." wrote my aunt. "That would've been so hard for Ken; he wasn't mean."

The reason was chillingly clear: One by one, enemy survivors were drawn into the vortex of water created by the behemoth screws of the submarine. One by one, the voices were silenced—except in my father's memory. He followed orders, did his duty, and paid forever. His peace of mind was a casualty of war, a victim of friendly fire. His deepest scar wasn't carved by the enemy, but by his own senior officer.

Many men died that day. Many others died a little every day afterward.

I judged my dad harshly for his bitterness toward Asian people. Now I suspect that in some desperate way he needed those victims to deserve their end.

He was searching for one thread of justification for an event that will never warrant that distinction.

Wedged in a lose-lose situation, the skipper was painted into a corner, and he made a costly, perilous judgment call. The buck stopped with him, on a small diesel boat with no room for passengers, too far from rescuers. If he gave up life rafts or supplies, he might cut his own crew short, and he couldn't afford to burn through ammunition they might need to defend the sub. It was an ugly wrestling match between brutal choices—to complete the aggression, or to submerge and leave men in a fiery aftermath with no hope of rescue. The water was frigid and shark-infested, and men were screaming and burning and drowning. Survivors who lasted long enough to be driven by thirst to drink seawater would go mad. Whatever his rationale, I'm sure the skipper's peace of mind was lost at sea that grim day.

This obscure act defines the phrase, "War is hell." Freedom is hard-won and dearly bought. Ask any veteran. Although my dad continued his military career, he left the sea behind. He completed his twenty years in the Air Force on land. He always taught me that the armed services defend our nation and deserve our respect.

Dad was all about respect—he showed it in the boxing ring, and it kept him from becoming a legendary contender in the Navy. Believe me when I say he had everything he needed to be the "last man standing." But when a boxing match came down to his opponent weaving in front of him while the crowd was yelling, "Finish him, finish him," there was something in my dad's soul that weighed in the risk of whether one more iron-fisted blow would leave the other guy a little bit punch drunk or worse. To him, a knockout just wasn't worth it; he didn't care about building an impressive stat sheet. Dad won, he knew it, and he walked away. Even when they begged him to keep boxing, he walked away. He was a respectful warrior and had his own boundaries.

That same respect came full circle at my father's funeral.

We were all stunned when he died at sixty-eight. His weary heart just refused to beat on.

Because my father was a veteran of three major conflicts—World War II, Korea, and Vietnam—one of the first calls I made was to McChord Air Force Base to request a color guard for his funeral at Willamette National Cemetery in Portland, Oregon. I wanted him to be buried with the dignity he'd earned during his career of military service.

The day of his funeral, I hoped to see a minivan of uniformed soldiers. But it wasn't there.

Instead, there was a full-sized military-blue bus. It was crowded.

The service passed in a blur of hot tears. But I can still see the face of the uniformed young woman who held the carefully folded flag that had draped my father's casket. The spent cartridges of the twenty-one-gun salute were tucked perfectly into the flag's triangular folds. Silent tears swept discreetly down her cheeks as she placed the flag into my silver-haired mother's trembling hands. This soldier hadn't known my father, and yet in some way, he was her comrade in arms. She saluted my mother in a studied, precise way that would've made Dad proud.

We've taken flowers to the cemetery often over the years and seen many funerals in progress. We've heard twenty-one-gun salutes and felt the swell of emotion when the lone soldier on the hill plays taps. But never again have we seen a color guard large enough to fill a bus. It was a poetic and fitting send-off for a man who had endured so much in the service of his country. It was a well-deserved tribute and honor for a man who spent his life picking up pieces of himself and living as a paler version of himself in the eyes of his family, who never fully understood. I hope other families of other veterans can learn and do better.

—Christy A. Caballero

True Identity

"Social Security number?"

It wasn't the first time I'd been asked that question, but it was the first since I'd become a military wife. My husband, Brian, and I had been married for a month.

It was also the first time I'd ventured this far without my new husband. Because I was new to the area, I'd had few outings without Brian as my escort. I barely knew how to find major places on post, like the commissary and the gas station. But now I'd found Dewitt Army Hospital by myself, and I was excited.

Smiling, I told the receptionist my Social Security number, so she could file my civilian medical records into the system. My feeling of accomplishment didn't last long. After a moment of staring at the computer screen, she looked at me sternly and said, "Your sponsor's Social, not yours." Feeling sheepish, I remembered my husband's instruction to memorize his Social Security number.

"You'll need it for everything you do on post," he'd said.

He was right. As I soon found out, everywhere I went, I was asked nothing about me and only about him: his branch of service, his Social Security number, his duty phone. Having been on active duty in the Army for almost four years before we married, Brian was already indoctrinated in military life. To prepare me for the culture shock, he'd explained as much as he could about military life—but he hadn't warned me about the emotions I was experiencing. I felt like no cared about me; they cared only about him . . . and his Social.

It was hard enough dealing with all the changes of being a newlywed. My husband and I had known each other for almost seven years before we were married, but living with someone is still an adjustment. Working through our likes and dislikes was interesting and even sometimes fun, but it also challenging, and I was still getting used to being a wife. Someone would call me "Mrs. Haynes," and it would take me a few minutes to realize they were talking to me. I had just moved from Baltimore, where I grew up, to Fort Belvoir, Virginia. I had left behind everything and everyone that was familiar to me and now had to make a long-distance call just to talk with my parents. Then there were all the new rules I had to learn about being a military wife. I had to get used to my husband stopping to salute soldiers who outranked him and to remember that the speed limits are considerably lower on military bases. My husband tried to make my transition easier, but I was still distressed. Now, the feeling that I was losing my identity made my new life seem overwhelming.

And it wasn't only receptionists and cashiers who seemed to look at me and see only my husband. While doing errands on base, I would run into my husband's coworkers at the PX or commissary, and though most of them were total strangers to me, they would approach me and say, "Hey, aren't you Sergeant Haynes's wife?" At first, it was a little confusing, because I didn't recognize them. But after it happened over and over again, for months and months, weariness set in. Each time, I'd smile and say yes, but my self-esteem was taking a beating. I knew they were not being malicious, but it still stung. I was losing another part of me.

It got to the point that when people would look at me with recognition and before they could say anything, I would say, "Yes, I'm Sergeant Haynes's wife." Meanwhile, inside, I was screaming, *My name is Terri! I do have an identity other than Sergeant Haynes's wife!*

Though, intellectually, I knew that the military is a place of honor and self-sacrifice, emotionally, I wasn't prepared for this type of self-sacrifice. I didn't realize I would lose something I had never even thought about before. I never imagined I would be identified as something other than myself.

Marrying into the military community can be strange for someone who is accustomed to conducting business in her own name and as her own person. I wasn't used to being identified by someone else's name, job, and rank. Part of me felt like I shouldn't complain about being called "Sergeant Haynes's wife," because it was a compliment to my husband. But I wanted to go back to being just Terri. I felt like I was being swallowed by a huge military world.

It was also a little strange that so many people knew me though I didn't know them. Sometimes I was greeted by people who didn't work directly with my husband; instead, they were people he had helped with their paperwork and forms, his customers. But the result was the same. The look, the smile, and the question: "Aren't you Sergeant Haynes's wife?" I started making it a point to tell people my first name, but on a base the size of Fort Belvoir, it was like mowing the lawn with a pair of kitchen shears.

This small attempt to regain my identity was a fruitless one, given that I never saw most of them again, and if I did, they didn't remember my name the next time anyway. All they did remember was that I was Sergeant Haynes's wife.

One day, while shopping in the PX, I noticed a man waving at me with the I-know-you look on his face. I thought to myself, *Here we go again.* Sure enough, he walked over and asked if I were Sergeant Haynes's wife.

"Yes," I said though clenched teeth.

"I thought so," he said. "I recognized you from the picture on his desk. He talked about you the whole time I was sitting there."

Mystery solved. That was the culprit: our wedding photo. The picture of the day I became Mrs. Terri Haynes; the picture that marked the beginning of the journey into my new life. In that moment, my irritation melted as I realized that people weren't overlooking my identity. My husband had made sure they knew exactly who I was—the woman he loved, the woman he had taken as his bride, the woman he had chosen to share his life with.

"Yeah, he tells everyone who comes to his desk about you," the man continued. "I could tell he really loves you."

It was a sobering moment. When I asked my husband about it, he confessed that he talked about me to anyone who would listen. He said my picture was the first thing anyone saw when they sat at his desk, including him. He wasn't letting people think of me as an anonymous dependent in a picture on his desk; instead, he was ensuring that everyone knew I was loved.

Six months later, my husband got promoted. As he stood before a crowd of his friends and coworkers, I got to hear some of the things he had been telling other people about me. During that ceremony, he said something that removed the last feelings of identity loss from my heart: "Coming home to Terri at night makes military life so much easier."

People still ask me "The Question," but that's okay. I know it's because my husband loves me and is not shy about letting people know how much. And when they ask, I proudly say, "Yes, I'm Sergeant Haynes's wife."

Now, if I could just get past being called "Dartanyon's mom."

—*Terri J. Haynes*

Day by Day

"She'll forget me," Herb said, cuddling our six-month-old daughter, Laura, to him. He touched her petal-soft cheek with his finger and watched her smile. "And she's going to change so much while I'm gone," he whispered with a sigh.

I blinked back tears, trying to be strong. "We'll write every day, and I'll send pictures."

He nodded. "I know, but it won't be the same as watching her learn to walk and hearing her first words."

Herb had received his orders for Vietnam, and Laura and I had a month to settle into my parents' home before he shipped out. After that, while Herb traveled thousands of miles away to live in a tent with strangers, our infant daughter and I would share my childhood bedroom.

My young husband and I wrapped our arms around each other, sheltering our baby girl in our embrace.

Our small family needed the comfort of oneness in an age of military conflict and youthful uncertainty.

On a chilly October morning in 1969, we traveled with our parents to the airport in Kansas City to see Herb off to his tour of duty. Laura was the only one of us who didn't cry on the way home. I envied her innocence and lack of understanding.

It took a few days to get into our new routine, but my parents were thrilled to have us in their home. Baby antics kept us busy, and the grandparent-child bond grew strong, a priceless gift for all of us.

Every evening when I got home from work, I flipped through the mail on the kitchen table, hoping to get a letter from Herb. Overseas mail often took a week or more, and when I received a letter or two, it was a special treat. Mail always meant a visit with Herb's family to share our letters. Laura loved the extra attention she received from grandparents on mail days.

"Send pictures and food," Herb wrote. "The Polaroids are fading with the heat and humidity over here."

Herb's grandmother and our mothers put together boxes to mail. I snapped more pictures of Laura, made a grocery list for snacks, and planned my next overseas package.

I remembered Herb's concern, "She'll forget me." I did everything I could to prevent that from hap-

pening. Every night when Laura got ready for bed, I
took the eight-by-ten photo of her daddy in his Army
uniform from the top of the television and held it
close for her to see. "Give Daddy a night-night kiss,"
I'd say, and she'd lean into the reflection and gently
press her mouth against the glass.

With Laura tucked snugly into her baby bed at
night, I wrote letters to Herb, outlining my day but
going into great detail describing Laura's. More teeth,
first steps, and a myriad of her newest words filled my
pages. As Glen Campbell sang "Wichita Lineman" in
the background, I struggled to keep my letters positive
and to not voice my fears about the war, but it was
hard. I was lonely, and I knew that even in his hectic,
overpopulated environment, Herb was homesick.

Grandparents, uncles, aunts, and cousins filled
my parent's home for Thanksgiving and Christmas.
My letters grew longer as I recounted the holidays
and described Laura's excitement at the sparkly lights
on the Christmas tree.

I traced her foot and hand on a sheet of paper so
Herb would see the change from baby fingers to little
girl prints. As days passed, Laura's accomplishments
stacked up like building blocks. "She loves to play
peek-a-boo," or "She walked across the living room
by herself," I wrote. Once I broke the news of her
stumble into the fireplace and the goose egg on her

head. If she said it, I told him. If she did it, I wrote about it. By the time her first birthday arrived, she was talking a blue streak. "I'm sixteen months and twenty-two pounds," Laura would say as she danced around the room. Her repertoire of nursery rhymes and songs entertained us daily, and I'd announce each new one learned in a letter to her daddy.

"You won't believe how smart she is," I bragged in one.

"I can't wait to find out for myself," Herb wrote back.

Summer passed into fall, and we excitedly began planning for Herb's return. I purchased a mobile home and fixed up a bedroom for Laura so she could get accustomed to sleeping in her own "big-girl" room. As October approached, I stopped writing letters but continued taking pictures to show him when he got home; mail wouldn't get delivered before Herb's return stateside.

Finally, the call came. "I'm in Seattle!" he shouted into the phone over the airport noise. We talked briefly before he said, "I'll see you in Kansas City."

Where I'd once been afraid that my anticipation of his return might jinx it, now the thought of becoming a family again threw my excitement into high gear. "Daddy's coming! Daddy's coming!" I sang, and Laura clapped her hands in delight.

It had been 367 days since our first trip to the airport. This time, only Herb's parents drove us to Kansas City. We waited at the gate, watching as passengers came through the walkway doors. Finally, there was Herb striding toward us, his gaze darting around the crowd seeking familiar faces. As our eyes met, I rushed into my handsome husband's arms. The young man who went to war returned as a seasoned traveler, an experienced soldier, and a wiser adult. Relief filled me at his safe return, but my heart was in my throat. It was impossible to speak, though I had so many things to say.

Herb's parents gathered around us, hugging and talking at the same time with Laura squeezed into the frenzy.

Finally, Herb pulled away and held out his arms to his daughter. "Hi, pretty girl," he said. The pride in his eyes was undeniable, the smile on his face fatherly tender.

We'd taken separation a day at a time. For Laura and Herb, getting reacquainted as parent and child would also be a day at a time, and we knew it might take a while. But at that moment, Laura went happily into her daddy's waiting arms.

"Give Daddy a kiss," I prompted. And she did, just like she had kissed his photo every night for a year.

—*Karen Gray Childress*

To Be the Son of a Soldier

There is a picture that has traveled with my family throughout the years, from Oregon to Indianapolis and across the Pacific to Japan. It hangs in my father's study in Germany now. The picture is of my brother, Timmy, and me, ages five and seven respectively. We are grinning inanely, ecstatically, freely. My brother has a plastic cup of root beer in his hands, and we both have foam moustaches. We are sitting on a red pleather couch, a bottle of ketchup in front of us. Those were the days of motel pools, sleeping together in beds we didn't have to make, diners, and roadside attractions as our family of four made our way from Oregon to Indianapolis.

We left La Grande, Oregon, in the winter of 1984. My dad had just completed Reserve Officer Training School at Eastern Oregon State University, and we were headed to Fort Ben Harrison in

Indianapolis. My dad was an officer now, and things were going to get better.

My brother and I were on a grand tour, delirious with freedom, away from classrooms with squeaky desks and bedtimes that interfered with life. We drank foreign substances and ate at Red Lobster and Wendy's. We stayed in hotels and chanted nonsensical rhymes to each other in the back of our beat-up, Army-green Toyota Corolla.

This wouldn't be the last time our family would take to the road. Eventually, we would circumvent the globe, posing by Billy the Kid's grave in New Mexico, acquiring a sister in Japan, and watching her go to college in Heidelberg, Germany. All of our trips have legendary tales and surreal moments, and those stories come out when the family reunites for holidays. But this story, this family heirloom, marks the first time I understood what it means to be the son of a soldier.

Driving an old Corolla across the Rocky Mountains in December didn't strike Timmy or me as foolish in any way. I vaguely remember my parents discussing the trip, but for us it has always been my father's word that settled matters. We set out from Oregon, crossing the desert and hugging the Snake River, following the Oregon Trail in reverse, through tiny towns and towering peaks. On the Oregon Trail, just as it crosses into Idaho, is a mountain pass called Dead Man's Pass, notorious for foggy winter nights and heavy snowfalls. This second leg of our trip would require a full day in the snow and plodding traffic. My brother and I were excited with the voodoo in the name of the pass. We widened our eyes at each other and burst into hysterical laughter. For my mother it was another matter altogether; her intuition flared up at the very mention of Dead Man's Pass.

According to legend, we were sitting in Sizzler's chowing on steak and potatoes when my dad and two cowboys struck up a conversation. The cowboys were rugged, in faded jeans and Stetsons, one bearded, the other clean-shaven. When they learned we were taking Dead Man's Pass, the clean-shaven one leaned in and whispered, "Some people head up into those mountains and never come back."

Stunned silence filled our table. The cowboy eased back in his chair and chewed his toothpick knowingly, nodding at us slowly. My dad, unflappable and with a strong sense of the ridiculous, started snickering uncontrollably. My mother began to wave her hands in agitation as she hurled questions at my father. Timmy and I returned to plates smothered in steak sauce and to tall cups of ice-cold Dr Pepper.

Later on, we listened as my mother sought assurances from my father for the rest of the night, while we tossed a Buffalo Bills plush-toy football around the hotel room.

Before we left the next morning, we stopped for coffee and breakfast at a local diner. My parents laughed about the cowboys from the night before, and my mom casually suggested they tie down the box atop our Corolla—the box filled with all the things we would need in Indianapolis before the movers arrived with the rest of our belongings.

My dad scoffed at her. "The thing weighs 5,000 pounds, woman!"

At this juncture, legend fades into myth, with versions differing across parental lines. My mom blames my father's irrational, stubborn nature. My dad asserts it was a technical error. The facts remain: My mother argued for strapping down the box; the box was not strapped down for the drive through Dead Man's Pass.

I remember driving at a snail's pace through the foggy winter day. A storm was blowing across the mountains, but it came silently, cloaked in snow. Time stood still in the darkened day, and it seemed like midnight to us. Two red taillights, floating in the milky-white haze several feet in front of our car, were our only link with civilization. I imagined a long train of silent, fearful automobiles, each following the other, holding hands in the darkness. I could feel the trust that linked us. I stared at the two red coals in front of our car and imagined the boy in the car behind us staring at his two coals. We whispered to one another in the silence, and even the wind blowing snowflakes across the Corolla was hushed. Massive eighteen-wheelers groaned past us, sounding hollow in the thick snowfall. No music played; only the muffled sounds of our winter caravan filled our dark car as we creaked along. It was slow going. Eventually, we all slept, except for Dad.

We emerged from Dead Man's Pass late in the evening and parked the Corolla in a Wendy's parking lot. The sky was grey, but the snow had stopped and begun to melt. As we stepped into the slush, we all looked to the top of our car—where a familiar shape no longer rested. When Timmy and I saw the look on our father's face change from shock to sheepish contrition, we giggled in anticipation of a good joke. But then we felt the whirlwind emanating from Mom. We sighed in mourning for the aborted joke and went into Wendy's to point at lunch.

The box was gone. We made it through Dead Man's Pass, but our belongings did not: clothes and toothbrushes for the trip, shoes and schoolbags for the first month in Indianapolis, and all of my dad's uniforms with the newly added lieutenant's bars on the shoulders. These facts did not dawn on us until we realized our pajamas were in the box. So were certain toys, whose disappearance we could scarcely contemplate. My mom gave a slow inventory of needful things lost in the snow of Dead Man's Pass, ticking them off on her fingers. The long drive through the fog and the shock of losing all of our possessions had rendered my father dopey. He swayed at the Wendy's counter as my mother continued with her list of doom. We ate in silence and found a motel.

The room was decorated in cheap Western décor, with floor-to-ceiling polyester curtains, fake wood paneling, and somber oil paintings of mountains and sunsets. My brother and I slept fitfully, me thrashing in my blankets and Timmy babbling in his sleep. My parents were up most of the night, rehashing the loss of the box and calculating the costs of refitting the entire expedition. They reached no conclusion and eventually lay on their backs on the motel bed, listening to traffic on the highway and watching the lights change color through the curtains.

In the morning, breakfast was postponed as my parents continued the debate they'd started the night before. They couldn't very well return to the pass, and any further delay might mean running into more storms, resulting in even longer delays. The only course of action was to carry on.

Unsatisfied with surrendering all of her posses-sions, my mother took charge and demanded that my father call the local authorities and report the miss-ing box. My father tried to console my mother into accepting that the loss was irrevocable. Mom was ada-mant; she wanted her home back, such as it was. She held out to the bitter end, and finally, Dad made the call to the local ranger station, if only to appease her.

"Umm, yeah, I don't suppose anyone has reported finding a box out there on Dead Man's Pass," inquired my dad. "It's a big box, has everything we own in it."

"Well, lessee here," drawled the ranger. "Whatchu say your name was?"

"Matuszak."

"Matuszak, huh? That wouldn't be Second Lieu-tenant Matuszak of the U.S. Army, would it?"

My father stammered something into the receiver. He looked at my mother in disbelief as he listened to the ranger. Then my parents rushed off to retrieve our belongings while my brother and I waited at the motel. When they came back, we cel-ebrated—Timmy and I, because celebrating was our business, and my parents, because they had their life back for the next couple of months.

The man who had found the box said he'd thought it was a car when he first spotted it along-side the road. When he realized it was a box, he was going to just leave it, but then he saw it belonged to an Army officer and that motivated him to bring it in to the ranger station.

I was awed. Our dad, who had been the goat for the last few hours, was Second Lieutenant Matuszak of the U.S. Army—respected and admired enough that absolute strangers would go out of their way to help him out. This was a momentous revelation for me. Our family had always been a self-sufficient bubble; "the Matuszaks" was my world. All the moving we did, and would do in the future, made our nuclear family indestructible yet also isolated at times. But I'd just learned that civilians—normal people—knew and understood what the bars on my dad's uniform meant.

That night we had a fine dinner at a swanky spot, and no matter how loud Timmy and I got, our parents just laughed.

I have always pictured the truck driver who found our box as a huge, burly man with a bushy moustache and a red baseball cap. He slams into a solid object somewhere in the fog of the pass. He climbs out of the cab of his eighteen-wheeler to inspect the car he thinks he's just hit and exclaims aloud when he sees it's a big box. He opens it up and looks inside, and his headlights shine onto a green uniform with the name "Matuszak" written in white on a black tag above the heart. He picks up the box, grunting, and throws it in the front seat, waving off the plaintive honks of the cars behind him. The trucker wipes snow off of the box and continues on toward town, smiling proudly as he wheels into the ranger station and drops off the officer's box.

And that is how Second Lieutenant Matuszak snatched victory from the jaws of doom, earning loving praise from his wife and hysterical cheering from his two sons. Farther down the road, the Corolla would break down in the vast fields of Nebraska; we would fend off giant cockroaches in a halfway house for incoming soldiers in Camp Zama, Japan; and we'd face disintegration in Frankfurt, Germany, when my dad's retirement forced our parents to re-evaluate life together. Every time, with every twist and pothole we encountered in our journey, my parents performed acts of extreme heroism.

My brother and I have remained largely as we were in that photograph taken twenty-five years ago in some truck-stop diner between La Grande and Indianapolis—oblivious and loving it. But when I walk past that picture, I can't help chuckling to myself . . . and thanking my parents for the fantasy tale of my childhood, a place filled with mythical quests and legendary heroes.

—Sascha Matuszak

Fate and Forgiveness

Without hesitation, he flipped up the rifle and pulled the trigger. The dog simply dropped. The others bolted at the sound of the gun. He didn't need to check the fallen dog; he knew it was dead. His main concern was the young calf that had almost been prey to the feral pack.

Slogging through the mud of early spring on his New Hampshire farm, Ray Fenner approached the shaken calf, head buried in the safest place he knew, near the hind leg of his mother next to her udder. The calf eyed the farmer suspiciously, fuming harsh breaths and releasing a brassy bleat; the intensity of the sound assured the calf was unharmed.

As the farmer moved toward the dog, the adrenaline began to wear off and the memory of a time long ago, when his reflexes had responded in a similar, though very different situation, began to emerge. He pushed the thoughts out of his mind.

He picked up the dog and carried it down the hill, where he dug a hole to bury it. As he looked at the dead animal one last time before shoveling the pile of wet dirt onto it, he remembered the books he had read as a boy about heroic dogs and their adventures. They had nobility and compassion that seemed to surpass that of most humans. How could such an honorable being become so vicious? Again, the memory started to push its way in. This time, he couldn't keep it away.

Toward the end of World War II, the Nazis had ravaged much of Europe, but the Allied forces were beginning to overpower them. After his first year of college studying to be a doctor, Ray joined the war effort; it had become clear every able-bodied young man was needed. After serving as a belly gunner and aerial photographer with the U.S. Army Air Corps, he was transferred to the infantry in Germany.

The liberation of the concentration camps had begun, and Ray and a platoon of soldiers were sent in to assist. When they had done all they could do to help the survivors, he and several others marched toward Belgium as the harshness of winter drew to an end.

Laughing as their boots kept getting sucked into the mud, they finally reached a sunny opening. A branch snapped nearby, and someone yelled "Get down!" just as shots rang out. Ray landed beside his buddy, and it took him a moment to realize that his friend had been fatally shot in the neck. Enraged, he stood up and fired aimlessly. Out of the corner of his eye, he caught a movement and swung his rifle. The helmet of the young Nazi soldier flew off as he fell backward. There was yelling, and what was left of the Nazi platoon began to retreat into the woods.

Ray lay shaking on the ground. He had shot a man—a man who had stood closely enough for him to see the youthful face, the frightened eyes. He rolled over and vomited.

When he could stand again, he looked across the clearing. The young man he had shot lay still, a bullet wound in the middle of his forehead, his pale blue eyes staring sightlessly skyward. Ray's stomach heaved again, but there was nothing left to expel. Slowly, he walked toward the man—a boy, really—and knelt down beside him. Tentatively, he reached for the soldier's hand and jumped back when he felt how warm it was. He'd never thought of death as being warm. He reached for the hand again and held it, fearing, but also wishing, that the soldier was not really dead and would suddenly grip his hand. When he didn't, Ray knew it was true. He had killed a man.

Shaking the scene out of his head, he reached inside the uniform of the Nazi soldier and found his dog tags. The name was Gerhardt Schmidt.

The somber group attended to the wounded and catalogued the dead. Three of their own had been killed. Many more of the Nazis had fallen, despite their advantage of surprise. Exhausted but unwilling to stay in this place, the U.S. soldiers picked up their gear and moved on.

As night fell, they came upon a cluster of houses somewhere near the border of Germany and Belgium. The village hadn't been touched by the war yet. Lights in the windows of the tiny houses almost made it possible to believe there was no war.

A man standing in a nearby doorway waved and began walking toward them. "May I offer you something to eat and drink?" he asked with a heavy accent.

Too tired and hungry to be wary, the soldiers gratefully accepted. They left their gear outside and followed the man into his home, warm and smelling of freshly baked bread.

"Where are you coming from?" asked the man as he offered them large chunks of bread.

Hardly able to speak as they shoved the food into their mouths, one of the soldiers managed to tell him that they'd recently arrived in Germany and were headed toward Belgium. The man assured them they had reached their goal.

Ray exhaled his relief. Between the aromas of the cottage and the kindness of their host, he felt tears sting his eyes. He looked away and tried to blink them back as the man handed him a glass and began to fill it with wine. The man looked into Ray's eyes and merely nodded as he moved on to the next soldier.

As he filled the last glass, he said, "I have no room for you to stay here, but there is a church next door where you might spend the night."

Sleepy from the bread and wine, the soldiers thanked the man for his hospitality. They picked up their gear, and the man led them into the dark church. He lit candles but soon extinguished them as the soldiers collapsed on the pews and fell almost instantly asleep.

Some time later, Ray groggily opened his eyes and looked across at a fellow soldier whose face was bathed in strange colors. Thinking that something must be wrong, Ray jerked his head up, but when he looked over the back of the pew he saw that the source of the odd sight was the morning sun shining through a stained-glass window. None of the others seemed to be awake yet, so he went outside.

"Guten morgen!" The man from last night called cheerily from next door as he swept his front steps. This morning he was wearing a black shirt with a white collar.

Ray waved and called "Good morning!" As he walked back toward the doorway, he stopped short and nearly choked. In the dark of the night before he hadn't noticed the sign on the front of the church: First Church of Christ, Reverend Gerhardt Schmidt. Surely, it couldn't be the same family! In a panic, Ray started to back away.

"Young man, is everything all right?" the man called.

Ray couldn't answer. He tripped over a root and fell to the ground as tears came pouring out.

The man walked quickly toward him and knelt down, taking Ray's hand in his. "My son, what is it?"

The sobs heaved so hard, Ray thought he'd be sick. "I think . . . I might . . . have killed . . . your . . . son." Ray tried again to run away, but the man's grip on his hand tightened. He pulled Ray toward him and wrapped him in his arms. Ray sobbed harder as the man rocked him slowly.

"Why don't you come inside, and I'll give you some breakfast."

The thought of food made Ray's stomach turn, but his energy to fight was gone, so he followed. The man silently poured them both some tea and sat down. A plate of sweet rolls sat on the table, waiting for the others to rouse.

"Why don't you tell me what happened?"

Ray took a deep breath and began to recount the story. The man closed his eyes as he listened; Ray saw a glint of wetness in the corners of them.

"You must hate me!" Ray blurted out and buried his head in his hands.

The man opened his eyes and turned, taking both of Ray's hands in his. "Look at me, son."

With great effort, Ray looked into the man's tear-stained face, the blur of his own tears distorting his vision. "You have done nothing wrong. You did exactly what you had to do at the time—defend your comrades against the enemy. It could as easily have been you who died, but that is the way of fate and the tragedy of war; it makes us do things that nothing else in the world could. Your willingness to put yourself in this position is noble."

Ray's hands were now trembling so hard he had to withdraw them. He wanted to say something but couldn't. Sensing Ray's dilemma, the man continued.

"Let me tell you about my son." He picked something up from a nearby table. It was a picture of the man's son a few years earlier, kneeling down next to a large dog. Recognizing the blond hair, the face that he had seen only in death, Ray hung his head and wept again.

"Young Gerhardt was a fine boy," the reverend said. "He was tall and strong like you. Though your hair is black, your blue eyes have the same intensity; I saw it when I looked at you last night. The pain in them conveyed what you have just told me. No man's eyes should ever have to look that way."

He took a deep breath and continued on, "Once, my family and I lived on a farm in a small village in Germany. Gerhardt loved the farm. He tended all of the animals with great care. After his mother passed on, he and I managed to take care of ourselves, though not as well as she had. Gerhardt always felt great responsibility for me.

"When Herr Hitler's ideas began to seep into the minds of the people, I decided we must move away from Germany. I could sense that very bad things were coming. We made it just in time, as it became much more difficult to do so after that. But my son had already begun to believe the propaganda of the Nazis and aspired to return to Germany as soon as he was old enough to join the Army. I begged him not to, but it was not my decision to make for him. His belief, perhaps like yours, was that he would be bringing honor to his people. I recently received a letter from him saying that he had begun to doubt his beliefs. Maybe he knew that he would never be able to live with himself when he found out how he and so many others had been deceived."

Ray's voice returned, and he said softly, "But now your son is dead because of me. Aren't you angry?"

"I am angry, indeed, but not with you—especially not with you. I am furious that young men, God's beautiful children, are being sacrificed to carry out or defend against the misguided ideas of a madman. My son has lost his life, but you have lost something that will be difficult to replace. Your task for the rest of your life will be to try to heal that part of yourself."

Voices in the distance interrupted the discussion. "My son, it is not my forgiveness you need—it is your own."

Ray remained in Europe for many months, and the war ended soon after his tour of duty was over, but something had begun that morning in Belgium. Though he would never see Reverend Schmidt again, the lesson he learned stayed with him.

After returning home, he finished college and then applied to divinity school with aspirations of becoming a minister. In addition to recounting this story, his application essay read, "If I have the opportunity to offer and teach this kind of forgiveness, then my life will be worth living."

As the farmer placed the final shovelful of dirt over the dog, he patted it down and whispered for the thousandth time, "Please forgive me."

Epilogue: My father recounted his story to my mother after the incident with the wild dogs because it shocked him that he was still such a good shot forty years after his military service in Germany. With the compassion of one who had received profound forgiveness, my father served as a Congregationalist minister for the rest of his life, working to help mend the soul wounds of others.

—Ellen Fenner

The Next Fifth Date

My husband has left for sea. Again. I rage against this absence as much as I did the first time the Navy called him away from me, a mere two years ago. When the door swings shut behind him and his stocked sea bag, the house and its occupants—me, the dogs, and the cats—are all left in a state of expectant waiting. Well, maybe not the cats so much, but for certain the dogs and me.

The dogs lurk around the house cautiously. Every extra noise is cause for concern, reason for a frantic race to the front door to investigate for potential intruders. It doesn't seem to matter if the source of their alert is merely the refrigerator kicking on. They are on constant standby. I can't say I blame them. Meanwhile, as long as the cats get their food, it truly doesn't seem to matter to them who is or is not in the house. For the rest of us, though, it makes for long days in which minutes can stretch into hours and longer nights, when neither the dogs nor I feel quite as brave when the refrigerator kicks on.

I know his mission is important. I know that my mission is to support him from home. But I dread every minute of it. So perhaps I am not a "good Navy wife."

Scott and I met and married in a whirlwind. I had finally found the love for which I had prayed so long. I had found my knight in shining armor. And what a knight! Scott is a compassionate man of strong morals, as dependable as the sunrise. (I realize this sounds a bit biased, but if you were to meet him, I am certain you would agree.) Marrying into the service did not give me a moment's pause. Truly, I would follow this man to the ends of the Earth and back again.

So I set out to do so. We moved 1,300 miles away from our friends and families, just as so many other military families have done. And, as countless other military spouses have done, since Scott deployed, I have single-handedly dealt with things like deceased vermin in the attic, locking myself out of the house, a lawn mower that wouldn't start, food poisoning . . . the list goes on. But above and beyond all of that, the worst thing I've dealt with is the loneliness.

You know the kind of loneliness I'm talking about. It's the ache in your heart when the only thing beside you in bed at night is a vast cold spot. It's the empty solitude you feel as you eat dinner by yourself. It's the silence and the absence of laughter in the home you've built together. It's realizing you've already accomplished the thirty suggestions your family support group gave you to help pass the time. It's going home to visit family and, upon arriving, realizing that although your world feels like it's ground to a standstill, everyone else's is still turning. It's checking your e-mail every ten minutes to see if he's written, afraid to leave the house in case he does. It's the four walls of that same house that seem to be falling in on you, swallowing you whole, making you almost crazy to escape. It's escaping the house to somewhere simple, like the mall, and realizing that even there, you are still the one walking alone.

But Scott and I have a secret antidote to the loneliness and challenge of living without each other while he's at sea. It's the one thing I hold onto, the one thing I use to get me through another night of televised canned laughter and a place setting at the table for one. It's the Rule of the Fifth Date.

Remember your first date? That anxiety of the night to come? Will he like me? Will she laugh at my jokes? Will we have anything in common to talk about? Now fast forward to your fifth date. You know you really enjoy his company. You may hold her hand, hug, share a kiss, and you breathlessly anticipate all of this with a glow that you simply can no longer hide. Scott and I have found that his every homecoming, no matter the length of his absence, is akin to our fifth date.

I plan for this reunion days in advance, carefully considering every detail: my clothing, my hair, the dinner, all of it. I gossip excitedly on the phone with anyone who will listen about my plans for his return. I bake his favorite dessert. The house is gleaming, the loneliness swept out to make room for the joy of his homecoming. When I know I am soon to be in his arms, my skin gets tingly, my heart gets fluttery, and my stomach jumps in excitement. I can't wait to see him, hear him, touch him, breathe him in again. Every time he comes home, it's our own kind of magic—as if we haven't been married, haven't been sharing our lives together, for more than two years. It's our fifth date all over again.

So now he is gone again, and I will protest, but only for a while. I know I have more important things to focus on, including our next fifth date. It's only a matter of time before we are seated together at our favorite restaurant, holding hands across the table, reveling in togetherness. We'll spend our time rediscovering what we missed while apart. We'll laugh at the pure joy that comes from being with your best friend again. And we'll begin the next day wrapped in each other's arms once more.

I can't honestly say that I don't worry about the days to come, when the sea bag comes back out of the closet and the stacks of black socks and white T-shirts dot our couch. But I can honestly say that while he is home again, and in my arms, we both strive to focus on basking in the quiet moments we make together, the moments in between. Next time he leaves, I will again object . . . at first. Then I'll look beyond the sadness of his departure to the joy of experiencing our next fifth date.

—*Nichole A. Gifford*

Such Purpose that Drives Them

Our son came home yesterday, and it was a good day. He took the airport floor in ten strides, eyes forward and that usual wide smile on his face. His arms were bulging—not from hours spent at an air-conditioned gym, as one might assume, but from the work he had done in a faraway land, in a war zone. His blond hair was lighter, and he looked as if he had grown an inch. I watched as he approached his father, grabbing his hand for a shake and wrapping his left arm around him. He didn't have to stand on his toes anymore to look Dad in the eye. I saw two bears posturing but with genuine affection for one another.

The intermittent e-mails he'd sent prior to his arrival had been our only contact for more than four months:

Hey mom im all good just got back again I was rolling through ***** when those convoys got hit im ok *we are all ok I love you and im back at the base I love you Peaches (me)*

Messages like those often came a day or two after a page-three article in the newspaper mentioning anonymous casualties in one short paragraph. Then the waiting game would start. We could breathe again when he reached a safe place and was able to let us know he was "all good."

He spent his entire tour on the road, which was actually a lot of white sand reflecting a blinding sun and making sunglasses a mandatory possession. So I always threw a new pair into his care packages along with new T-shirts, beef jerky, candy, music, pictures, and lots of Silly String. Anything to make him smile as he wove his way through the "sandbox." The bulk package of gummy bears was almost a joke, he said, because it had to go in one shot or it would have melted. He was glad to share, anyway, because there were plenty of guys who never received any mail.

I didn't really start crying until this morning when he asked for more eggs. More eggs.

His shirt tan, buffed physique, and a new smoking habit are the only remaining signs of convoy duty in all the "hot zones." One full night of food, laughter, and friends wanting to try on his helmet and vest, and he finally passed out. I watched him sleeping on the couch with his feet hanging over the edge.

He said very little about his tour, and we cautioned some of his friends not to ask, but my husband and I were already aware of some of the details. One of his naïve buddies found an orange plastic cap gun in the dining room and popped one off behind him. He just turned around with that boyish grin and asked the guy to put it away. He sat in the center of his college friends, and they gave him space, prodding and joking with him as they had done in high school. But I could see they were watching him, just as we were, all of us eager to subtract anything bad from his experience, if we were able.

After the barrage of visitors, the really good part came. The three of us sat in the kitchen talking. My son pulled out his wallet and showed us all of the driving certifications he had gained. He could operate just about anything with wheels, just like Dad. He took his boots off, and the sight of his feet, hard as cement from the hot ground, sent me running for a bucket of warm water and Epsom salts. They both laughed at me.

Then he spoke of the road and driving with a 9mm on one leg and an M-16 beside him. It was his job to move people and supplies from one location to another. For safety, the destination was a living thing that changed from moment to moment. The radio gave him every instruction, and his convoy moved with speedy efficiency to get to the next checkpoint. If they were ordered to stop for blessed sleep, they would dig beds in the ground and one guy would stand guard. His helmet was his wash basin, food bowl, and friend.

Anyway, the real reason I'm telling this story is to mention another important thing I noticed yesterday. It struck me as I watched father and son talking out in the back yard. I had not realized until then how quiet my husband had been. His comments are usually matter-of-fact, and he generally tends to let the other voices sing first. There had been much "singing" yesterday.

All of our company had left, and my two guys drifted outside to talk. I saw lots of nodding and an occasional smile, but I could not hear the conversation.

My husband knew our son had met the devil on the road, just as he himself had done several times during his own truck driving career. Each of them had seen things that were not necessarily conversational material, and I think they were exchanging some of those things. Bad things can take on different forms. My husband's were often the view of a really bad wreck or a hard-knuckle drive in a whiteout. Our son's may have been the sight of a guy on the roadside selling strands of some kind of meat and holding an AK-47. I know I will never hear some of the information they exchanged that night, but I'm really glad my son talked to his dad.

Anyway, when I walked outside to bring them some drinks, I noticed this single remarkable thing: Our son was wearing his father's plaid flannel jacket, and it hung on his strong shoulders in an equal fashion. Each of them had a short haircut, only my husband's was that great silver color he loves to be teased about. Otherwise, I was seeing double. That one inch of height I thought our son had gained was due only to a correctness of posture he had acquired. Our boy had become a man, and he had come home tired, hungry, and full of new memories, just like his dad. Though they had driven in different lands and under different circumstances, they had faced the difficulties and dangers of the road with the same courage, diligence, and pride.

And I am so proud of the two of them. I can't write enough stories or fry enough eggs to show that. But from watching them, I clearly understand one thing now. Everyone just wants to do his job and come home. That's what it's all about, isn't it?

—*Julie A. Whan*

This story was first published in Truckers News *magazine, February 2008. It has been edited for publication in this book.*

The World in My Hands

Like all things, growing up in the military had its pros and cons—or yin and yang, if you prefer. Because my father chose a career in the military, I did not get to experience certain things as a child. I didn't get to grow up with my grandma and grandpa living down the street and visiting every Sunday for supper. I have cousins I've never even met. I didn't have lifelong childhood friends. I never had a sense of community or knew what to say when people asked me where I was from. It seemed an odd question. "You mean, where we lived last, or where we lived first, or where we lived the longest?"

As a member of Canada's Air Force, my father went to Africa, Pakistan, Europe, and the United States. He told me stories about droughts, epidemics, and delivering food to starving people. He was my hero. He explained to me about political unrest, racism, riots, and peacekeeping. Could there be a more noble way to spend one's life? I learned to fear Russia and the potential threat it held at the time. I listened in earnest to stories about hunting subs in the Atlantic and about polar patrols. It made me feel secure knowing that someone was sitting on a wall and personally keeping me safe.

I remember my father returning from foreign places and the money and coins he would bring home for me. They all had weird-looking, foreign, mysterious markings and faces or pictures. I memorized those coins and loved them, imagining they were exotic treasures. I looked up the countries in encyclopedias and dreamed about what the places were like, imagining the day when I would get to go, too.

I was going to be just like my dad. I was going to join the military. I was going to sit on a wall and travel the world at the same time.

I was eleven before I actually realized there were jobs other than being in the military. Honest.

It's not that we never left the various military bases where I grew up. Sure, we went shopping at regular stores where civilians worked. We drove past factories and offices where civilians worked. Though I had a sense that people worked there, I figured all those jobs were being done by the husband or wife of a military person, to make a little extra cash for their family. I never thought of them as actual professions. As a child, that was my reality.

Then, when I was eleven, my father bought a house off base and I changed schools. For the first time, I had a friend who wasn't another base brat. When I asked what her father did, she told me he worked at a printing company. Then I asked her what rank he was, and she looked at me like I was an idiot.

"Well, is he like a private or more like a five-star general?" I asked, trying to put things into terms I could grasp.

"He's, like, a printer," she explained slowly. "They don't have ranks."

I was shocked. How could the world exist without ranks? How do you know who the boss is? Who do you salute?

Four years later, I acquired my first non–base-brat boyfriend. His dad was a farmer, with cows and barn cats . . . and a pony! A real live pony! I'd never known anyone with a pony.

He showed me around his giant farmhouse and pointed out all the places of interest. "This is the window I put my head through when I was six, trying to roller skate with my feet tied to old Tonka trucks."

"You've lived in this house since you were six?" I asked in utter shock.

"Um, I've lived in this house since I was three days old," he told me with that same you-are-an-idiot look I recognized from my friend with the printer-dad.

At that point in my life, I was sixteen and had already lived in eight different houses. I looked all around and thought how very strange it was to live in the same house for sixteen years. Little did I know that in ten years I would marry this man or that we'd later live in the house next door for twelve years.

I'm all grown up now, and I never joined the military. Instead, I went to school and got a degree in international marketing and personnel management. This is one area of my life in which growing up military has paid off, enabling me to develop certain skills that have served me well in my chosen profession. I have traveled around the globe completely, in both directions, without fear or hesitation. Neither a crowded Tokyo airport, nor a fully armed Israeli security check, nor a combination of lost passport and missing suitcase can scare me.

The yang of growing up military has played out in my personal life, too. A social chameleon, I can slip into any social setting easily and comfortably. Being forced to meet new people each year, when either your friends moved or you did, really hones your skills at meeting and integrating with people. I am never lonely.

I don't have a sibling within three time zones, but we are all still very close and involved in one another's lives, even if we don't do Sunday suppers. I understand that "home" is not a geographic location but a place in your heart.

My father has retired and the tables have turned. Now, I'm the one who travels for work or just for fun and brings home coins—except I don't let him keep them! He only gets to look. Then he has to give them back, so I can add them to my collection—the one he started for me forty years ago.

I've met some former brats who are bitter or angry that their parents chose a career in the military. They're angry that they don't have a hometown or lifelong childhood friends. I just don't get it. My father brought me the world, one piece at a time. He dropped it into the palm of my hand and then gave me the tools to go out and see that world for myself. To me, any dot on a map is just a ticket and a nap away. I've been to Cairo. (Dad told me not to drink the water. I didn't listen. Really should have.) I've been to London. (Dad told me I wouldn't like the food. I didn't listen. Probably should have.) I sleep like a baby on airplanes because my daddy used to fix them when I was a little girl. (Dad told me they were safe. I listened. I'm so glad I did.)

—*Allison L. Maher*

One Veteran's Story

My husband, Bruce, was twenty-five in June of 1967, when the U.S. Army drafted him during the Vietnam War. Finished with grad school, he was teaching in Connecticut and had plans to marry in three months—not to me (I was a sophomore in high school) but to a girl he'd met in college.

Deciding he'd rather be the one giving the orders than taking them, he enlisted in the Marines and made plans to go to Officer Candidate School. Then he told his fiancée what he'd done and gave her the option of postponing the wedding, knowing he could be killed or maimed. They married as planned.

The thirteen months he spent in the jungles of Nam are not something he's said much about. I've seen his medals. I've seen the Vietnam flag he pulled from an enemy stronghold somewhere. I've read letters from superiors praising the job he did.

But I know little. It was hot. He made sure his men were taken care of. He made decisions for the greater good. He gave orders that impacted lives. He saw his men get killed. He wrote letters to their parents back home.

The rest he's buried deep inside somewhere. I don't know if he thinks of it much, but he winces at the whir of helicopters overhead, recoils sharply at the sound of gunfire, and is moved to tears watching war movies.

"Did any of your men commit the atrocities we heard so much of?" I asked once, naively and, in retrospect, perhaps thoughtlessly.

"No," he said simply.

"How do you know?"

"Because I was with them," he told me.

I became silent, taking in all that this said about my husband.

Bruce didn't want to fight in that war, but running to Canada's open border was not for him. He was an American and would face the cards he was dealt head on. Enlisting and training to become an officer pretty much ensured that he'd be in the thick of things in the steamy jungle half a world away. And he was.

He survived, although many he knew did not.

He cried at the Vietnam Veterans Memorial in Washington, D.C., years after he returned to civilian life.

The welcome home was anything but. He told me that when he returned from Vietnam, he was spat on at the San Francisco airport.

Recently, four decades after that homecoming, an invitation arrived by e-mail. Some members of his class at Officer Candidate School in Quantico, Virginia, are planning a reunion. We'll go.

As a veteran, what does my husband want? Absolutely nothing . . . except maybe acknowledgment that he did what he was trained to do to the best of his ability. He followed orders and, in turn, gave them. He served his country as required.

But it was war, and what is it good for?

A few evenings ago, Bruce and I sat on the patio at dusk, rehashing the day.

It had been beautiful. The weather had cooperated for our son David's high school graduation, which was a milestone for me as well as David. He's the youngest. We'll soon have an empty nest, temporarily, at least, while he's away at college. I think this will be fine. I've looked forward to it. And yet . . .

"Are we going to the parade tomorrow?" I asked Bruce. "Tomorrow" was Memorial Day.

"I suppose," he said.

I mentioned that there would be a ceremony at each of the cemeteries in town. Taps would be played in honor of the dead who'd served our country in war.

"That would be tough for me," he said.

"It would be too emotional?" I asked carefully.

When I first met Bruce, I'd tried to get him to talk. I felt shut out. What had happened? What was it like? Why could he not share with me? I loved him. I would never hurt him. I could share his pain. He wouldn't talk. He couldn't. I had let him be . . . for years.

But that night he seemed open. So I asked what it was that, after all these years, made it so difficult, not just for him but for so many other veterans, to speak of their war experience.

The question was like a grenade that split the air between us. My husband accused me of tossing it, but I hadn't even known I'd held it, let alone pulled the pin.

He made it clear in no uncertain terms: This was a subject he wanted to remain buried. I need to understand. I'm not to ask questions. He won't answer them. It isn't that he doesn't trust me to be gentle. Yes, it might help if he talked, but he won't. Or he can't.

With that, he got up and went into the house.

I sat alone. He had every right to keep his experience to himself, but I felt hurt. His hurt was bigger, though; I'd swallow mine. What choice did I have?

Then he returned. Sitting in the soft evening light, he spoke haltingly of learning that survival meant making decisions, quick ones, life-or-death ones. He said sometimes those decisions were made "for the greater good." Those who couldn't make decisions got men killed. He said he was in charge of his men; it was his responsibility to bring them through alive. But some didn't make it.

We sat silently watching the goldfinch at the feeder. I changed the subject.

The next day, we went to the town common for a simple Memorial Day ceremony. We stood with others in front of the memorial engraved with names of local men who'd died in wars from World War I to Vietnam. It was like all the small-town ceremonies held across the nation. Dignitaries spoke. Veterans spoke. There was a gun salute and a bugler.

I stood beside Bruce. I was grateful his name was not on the monument. He began wiping silent tears long before the bugle blew taps. I put my arm around him and hoped some of his pain drained with each tear. That was all I could do. Perhaps it was enough.

—*Ruth Douillette*

The Spouses Club

They wait. Some of the kids are old enough to know what they are waiting for; others, sitting in repose on their mother's laps, are not. Under the hot Alabama sun, the sweat from the mothers' legs slips against the babies' legs as they doze in the heat. It's late now, but the heat of the South is relentless, and as long as the sun is up the temperature stays high. A full day of play has plastered the children's hair to their foreheads in dirty, matted clumps, but, resilient, they continue to play.

The playground where they play and wait is in front of the buildings that lodge the airmen who are temporarily stationed here. For those who bring along their wives (or husbands) and their kids, as many do, the entire family spends those five weeks in a bare-bones housing unit designed for one airman.

The quarters don't seem so bad at first—until the wives try to live in them while their husbands are gone all day, training and working. Soon, one dresser doesn't seem like enough for one person, let alone a family. And no air conditioning seems like a cruel joke. Trying to find places for shoes and toys seems frustratingly futile. Trying not to work up a sweat while washing the handful of dishes stocked in the kitchenette quickly becomes tiresome. The playground is the only place to go.

So the wives spend most of the day at the playground, talking, laughing, and sharing. This is where they share any extra towels housekeeping left in their room or the serrated knife a former resident left behind in another. They watch all the children, not just their own, on the jungle gyms; no one need worry about running off to the bathroom or to switch a load of laundry, avoiding the machine without a spin cycle. And they share the wait as the end of the day slowly nears—the end of their spouses' workday that inevitably comes later than they were assured it would.

The women and children trickle in and out of the playground all day long, working around naps and lunch and trips to the store. The kids go crazy cooped up in the rooms. When they're not eating or sleeping, they bang on the door, pleading to go out. But the playground is as much a release for the mothers as it is for the children.

All of the women have come here to this training camp to spend time with their husbands. In the high ops tempo of the Air Force, deployments and TDYs are as commonplace as being home, where they're officially stationed. When a five-week stint in one place or another comes up, although bringing your spouse is discouraged, it is certainly allowed. Understandably, forty-four members have brought their spouses to this training trip—including two female airmen who've brought their husbands.

While the members of class 08-D train all day to become better officers, their spouses unofficially train all day to become better military spouses, an exercise that they've been practicing since the day they wed. They learn where the commissary is on this base, what days it's closed, and to tip the baggers. They learn which spouses have kids here and which don't. They learn which housekeepers will come early and which will work around the kids' naptimes. They learn how to navigate the stairs to their rooms with a baby in one arm and three bags of groceries in the other.

Without a complaint, the ten-by-ten-foot room quickly becomes home. The wife finds a place for shoes above the refrigerator and for coats in the cabinets over the stove. The toys are stored under the desk, and the toiletries are lined in rows on the back of the toilet. Meals are made on mini-stoves, and then eaten alone most days.

As each day wears down, the playground begins to crowd. All the wives come there to wait. They wait for their husbands to pass through on their way home—their home for five weeks, the hot, cramped lodging room.

As the wives watch their children play and talk amongst themselves, they keep an eye on the road for their husbands. Each uniformed airman approaching from a distance is scrutinized for a telltale gait—the only identifying characteristic, when everyone is dressed alike, that tells a wife from afar that her husband is approaching. One wife is married to a special operations officer, the only one who wears a red beret. She can identify her husband from the masses from a greater distance than the rest, and when she sees him coming she shouts to her daughter from across the playground, "Erin, I see a red hat!"

The women dig their bare feet into the woodchips under the picnic tables, wriggling their toes, wondering who will be led away first. Lined up along the benches and at the tables, the women look not unlike the girls sitting along the bleachers at a high school dance, waiting to be picked for a slow song.

The chatter of the day dies down as the evening approaches and everyone's thoughts turn to the brief reunion they've been waiting for with such patience and longing. As each husband returns, a heart beats faster and expands with love while another one breaks a little. Although the wait will be only another few minutes, it's been a long time apart already. Long days seem all the longer when you are away from home.

Some of the wives don't have a home to return to. Some have packed up all their belongings and are moving to a new base, to a new home yet unknown to them. Some of them wait all day for an embrace and a short conversation before he changes clothes and goes off to study for the next day's lessons. Some hold onto these precious moments at the end of the day for all they can, knowing that at the end of these five weeks their husbands will be sending them back home, kissing them goodbye at the airplane terminal, and deploying.

When the last husband trudges home, his wife is anxious but is never waiting inside . . . or alone. Although the second-to-last airman to arrive home may have reached the playground ten or more minutes before, he has not managed to lead his family upstairs to their tiny quarters yet—because his wife has started a conversation with the last remaining wife. An artist at keeping the conversation going, she has managed to push words back and forth, twisting and pulling questions out of the air until she's nearly exhausted, all for the sake of not leaving the last wife alone to wait.

The next day will be the same. The wives, no matter how early their babies wake them, will wake to an empty room. After dressing and feeding their children, they will take them outside to play. At the playground, they will meet the other wives, where they will talk, sharing with and supporting one another as they wait for their partners and those precious moments between this long, hard day and the next one.

—Rachel McClain

Home Is Not a Place for Me

There are three questions people ask when we first meet that stymie me:

"Why are you still single?" (My response: *Why are you still married to that horror?*)

"Are you a natural blonde?" (*Are you a natural moron?*)

"Where are you from?" (*Uh, how long have you got?*)

That last one is a reasonable question to which there is no simple answer. Sometimes I just say "Massachusetts," because that is where I happen to live at the moment and the Red Sox rule. Sometimes I just say "New Orleans," because of all the places I lived during my formative years, I love that place the most and you can still get a drive-through Daiquiri there. And sometimes I just say "California," because that's where I lived the longest and, well, it's California.

What I never say is the truth, which would be, "Nowhere. I'm an Army brat." If I know people long enough, eventually they find out, and I brace myself to be judged, stereotyped, and ultimately, misunderstood.

"You must have been a lonely child." (*I'm the only writer I know who had a happy childhood.*)

"Your father must have been tough on you." (*At least I like my father.*)

"All that moving around must have damaged you." (*Apart from making me flexible, worldly, and tolerant, you mean?*)

This stereotype of the lonely, overparented, perpetual new kid on the block runs rampant among, as my father always says with a slight sneer, "civilians." True, most of us may sometimes feel, as fellow brat Pat Conroy once put it, "desperate" for a hometown. But that desperation is often outweighed by a sense of adventure.

For military brats, hometown is a moving target. From Georgia to Germany, Oklahoma to Ohio, Kansas to North Carolina, Indiana to Louisiana, my hometown shape-shifted as my mother and I bounced along with my father from post to post: armed camps atop foreign mountains, sweltering cities in the swampland, hick towns flanking dried-up river beds, suburbs lost in fields of yellow corn.

I couldn't name them all—I know because I once took a writing course in which I was required to try.

Now, as a bookish writer living the most ordinary of civilian lives in small-town New England, I don't come across many fellow military brats. When I do, it's like coming across a fellow countryman while abroad. You are strangers, yes, but united in culture, history, and the mother tongue. Whether you like each other or not, it is comforting to connect with people whose zeitgeist echoes yours.

You speak the same language—reveille at oh-six-hundred-hours. You share the same history—scrambling around on tanks on field day, stopping in your tracks at sundown while the flag comes down, starting each movie with the "Star-Spangled Banner." You laugh at the same jokes—Charlie Sheen in *Hot Shots*—and glisten (not cry, wimp, glisten) at the same cathartic moments—Charlie Sheen in *Platoon*. You get the same cultural references: chafing dishes, in country, The World. And no matter how brief the encounter, you part as fast friends, thanks to a kinship that runs as deep as any found among those from the same hometown.

Military brats make fast friends—fast. We don't have the luxury of time. We know we might move tomorrow—or will. Being from a big family helps. As an only child, I envied them—those kids had siblings to play with until they made their own friends. I was alone with my mother and my father, who entertained me as best they could whenever we found ourselves in a new place. (Summer was the worst because there was no school. School meant kids, and kids meant friends. I loved school.) My father usually disdained the sorts of games that amused children—cards, Scrabble, charades. But whenever we moved, he'd sit down with my mother and me and play euchre. This euchre-playing lasted about a week, by which time I was supposed to have acclimated myself like the good soldier I was.

My mother was shy, and for her it must have been a lonely life at times. With my father off in Korea, Vietnam, and God knows where else ("That's classified"), she was often alone with me for months, sometimes years, at a time. Her reserve hampered her ability to make friends—and she didn't want me to suffer the same friendless fate. So whenever we moved into new quarters on a new post, she'd send me outside on that terrible first day.

"Don't come back until you've made a friend," Mom would say.

And propelled by my mother's little push, I'd find myself out on the street, looking for kids my age. I'd stumble around until I found one. I knew where to look. There were always boys playing war in the woods, girls swinging on the swings at the playground, and everyone swimming in the nearest body of water—be it pool, creek, or sprinkler.

I'd position myself in the middle of the crowd of kids and just hang around until the opportunity presented itself, and then I'd start talking.

Brats like me jumped in; they were as eager to make friends as I was. Civilians took longer, but sooner or later one of the less popular kids would cave and I'd drag 'em home to my house for my mother's pecan pie. Between my mother's superior baking skills and my elevated status as an only child with lots of toys and no pestering siblings, I always made it home with a new friend by dinnertime.

That is not to say I didn't sometimes wish we would stay put—at least for a couple of consecutive school grades. But as much as I may have longed for a hometown as a child, when I grew up and could have made my own, I didn't. As an adult I've moved nearly as often as we did when I was a kid. And I've loved every place, each in its own way.

Your true hometown is your childhood, and I carry mine with me wherever I go. Mine was not a military gothic, Pat Conroy–style childhood. There was no Great Santini in my life; my father was—and remains—an officer and a gentleman, through and through. My mother was the perfect colonel's wife—and perfect mother, perfect grandmother, and soon-to-be perfect great-grandmother. Mine was an idyllic—if nomadic—experience, full of love and laughter and lots of John Philip Sousa music.

Growing up in the military is like sex or childbirth or combat—you have to experience it to understand it. So the next time someone asks me where I'm from, I'll just say, "Nowhere. And everywhere."

Because we military brats grow up knowing that it's not where you're from that matters, it's where you are going . . . and the friends you make when you get there.

—*Paula Munier*

You *Are* the Mom

Departure ceremonies for National Guard soldiers demonstrate some of what freedom requires. Young fathers cry openly as they hand back babies to wives. The children who are old enough to understand what is happening sob as the dad they need to lead them through their adolescence disappears in the distance. The wives stretch one arm to embrace a convulsing child while the other arm clutches a sheaf of papers telling her "How to Avoid Eviction"—since, for many, the resulting cut in pay will be more than they had been told to budget for originally.

Afterward, little yellow ribbons flutter forlornly in the breeze. The silence is deafening. Most of the crowd quietly disperses. A few stand frozen in the parking lot, staring down the empty road where the bus has disappeared, unable to move toward an uncertain future.

Every day for the next year or more, every one of those left behind will turn onto the street that leads home, with sweaty palms gripping steering wheels and hearts pounding in throats—wondering if uniformed chaplains will be standing at their door.

I know this. I am the mother of a soldier.

When my son first told me of their mission to clear weapon caches in the mountains of Afghanistan, I simply sat down—for days—unable to move. Friends called, and I could not answer the phone. Once or twice I sat at the computer to write my thoughts but could not keep my fingers on the keyboard. In my nightmares, whenever I finally did sleep, Bryan was two years old, lost and hurt. I could hear his cries, but I couldn't find him. In my waking hours, the thought of his being beyond my aid made me nauseous. Although I believed that the terrorist camps in Afghanistan needed dismantling, I was terrified for my son's safety.

Gradually, I began to feel that if he could summon the courage to go, I could summon the will to bear it. As he stood taller, so did I. He moved with strong, calm, clear-eyed focus. I made long lists of things to do for him while he was gone: bills to pay, car to sell, condo to rent. We would get through this. As a soldier and as the mother of a soldier, we would do our duty. Then he would come home, and all would be well. And so we did.

Phone calls, the Internet, packages, and pictures filled the days. Prayer filled the nights. My friend Mattie held me together over the phone lines in the middle of the night. "God is holding Bryan in His mighty hand," she would assure me. The complete and certain faith in her voice made functioning possible.

Only once did I break down crying—while trying to pack a decent birthday cake to mail him on a cold, icy day in January. It was his favorite, strawberry, but without fresh berries and with canned icing still in the can. The cake itself had to be packed in the baking pan, a pathetic shadow of the three-tiered, decorated pastry I so wanted to provide. As I wiped my tears, I comforted myself by remembering that, as a boy, Bryan had enjoyed high-risk sports like snowboarding and rock climbing. Using both his physical agility and astute mental instincts, he had never been hurt. I told myself he would come home okay this time, too. And he did.

Fortunately, Bryan did not tell me about his more harrowing experiences—the rocket attacks, the bullets hitting his helicopter, narrow roads ending on the edge of mile-high cliffs, caves and ambushes— until he was where I could see that he was truly all right. Then he enclosed a note in a beautiful card: "Thanks, Mom, for all your support. I couldn't have done it without you."

Life gradually returned to normal—work, soccer, friends, holidays. Two years went by. Soon his commitment to the National Guard would be over. Then he invited me to a coffeehouse visit, something we occasionally did as a convenient place to chat.

"We're being deployed to Iraq in three months," he broke the news.

"No!" I reacted as though I had been struck. I stood up. "You've done your part. Don't go! Iraq is a stupid war—a mess that never should have started."

"Mom, I have to. I'm a soldier." Bryan lowered his voice and looked around. "Please, Mom. Sit down."

"It's not going to happen," I said, gathering my things. "Something will change it. You'll see." And I left.

For the next several weeks I remained in denial. If the subject came up, I'd say in a breezy, confident tone, "You're not going." Bryan would just roll his eyes and change the subject.

When I learned that his mission in Iraq would be as a squad leader guarding convoys, my heart sank. No amount of physical agility and astute mental facility can defend against an IED.

Fully packed and ready to go, Bryan reported to the departure site four days before the ceremony, as required. Then he called us. The Army doctor had blocked his deployment. He had a damaged hamstring from a year-old soccer injury that would not support the 100 pounds or more that infantry soldiers often carry.

Feeling as though I'd suddenly begun to breathe pure oxygen, I phoned family and friends. "He's not going! He's not going! Oh, thank God!"

Bryan and I met at the coffeehouse again. But his face did not reflect the joy that shone from mine. Looking stricken, he relayed the details of his return.

Ignoring these facts, I addressed his feelings. "I don't understand," I said. "This is an ugly, senseless war . . . I protested it from the start . . . Almost nobody believes in it anymore."

"It's not about that, Mom," he said, his eyes finally squinting annoyance. "It's about our commitment to each other. There are younger men who've never been in combat who were counting on me to lead them . . . and to bring them back." Mercifully, the rest was not spoken out loud: They have mothers, too.

I dropped my gaze as my cheeks grew hot.

Later, my intuitive sister simply said, "Don't feel bad about being the mom. You *are* the mom."

Yes. Yes, I am.

—*S. Ann Robinson*

Hero in the House

"You need a good father figure in the house," my mother told my brother, sister, and me after she married our stepfather. But that wasn't the only reason she married him; she really did love him. Though she had dated guys on and off for the past few years, I'd never seen her act like she was this much in love with any man. You would have thought they were two infatuated teenagers, but there was something deeper between them, too—an invisible but palpable connection that said they had a lot of respect and compassion for each other and were will-ing to make it work.

We gave him a hard time whenever we could, and it often put her in the middle. But he was a Vietnam veteran, had trained recruits in the military for service in the Vietnam War, and had handled just about any type of insubordination you could think of. So even the cleverest tactics we came up with for disrupting the status quo were small potatoes to him.

We weren't mean kids. We were good kids who resented having a stepfather around.

And he wasn't a mean stepfather, just strict. This came from being a soldier; my sister and I were sure of it. We had heard about battle fatigue from educational television shows and at school, and so our young cynical minds diagnosed and analyzed his every word and move. At that point, he had been in our lives only a few months, and we weren't used to strict rules. How long was this going to last? How long was their marriage going to last?

"You're grounded." My stepfather said this to my sixteen-year-old sister when she sneaked out of the house to go riding around with older friends in their car. I was nineteen at the time.

Grounded? She had never been grounded before. Mom was always one who talked things out with us, lectured us, looked the other way, or just let it slide. We weren't used to restrictions.

"For a week," he confirmed. And Mom backed him up.

A week of staying inside in her room?

"He is a time bomb," I told our mother.

"No," she said. "He's trying to teach her a lesson."

What did she see in him, anyway? Sure, he was nice-looking and soft-spoken, but why would she want somebody so bossy? Surely she could see this overzealous Vietnam vet was taking away our freedom.

"She did something she wasn't supposed to," Mom told me.

She was actually defending him.

"How can you take his side?" my sister asked her.

We felt like we were being betrayed a little bit by our mother as well.

It had been just the four of us for several years now, no father figure to tell us what to do. Our younger brother rarely got into trouble. He was thirteen and easygoing, a kid who kept to his curfew. He didn't complain about our stepfather as much as my sister and I did, but he was a little resentful too. He was no longer the only man of the house.

I watched sadly as my sister was confined to her room each night after school. She could eat dinner in her room, of course, and come out to go to the restroom, but she couldn't use the phone, talk to company, or go anywhere.

My sadness turned to anger, and I decided on the very first night to be grounded with my sister. So I exiled myself to her room each night too, and we sat and talked on the bed about how unfair it was and how mean he was and how shortsighted Mom was for going along with his plan to discipline us. Is this what a military family was supposed to be like? Full of rules, regulations, harsh consequences? If so, we wanted no part of it.

We weren't always complaining and fussing with him, though. A lot of times he could be really funny and compassionate, and he liked to teach us things and tell us stories about hunting or growing up with a houseful of siblings. But usually we were standoffish with him, trying to keep him as far away from our daily lives as possible.

Then, one day about a month after my sister's grounding, I was given the job of vacuuming out all the closets. Of course I complained, wondering why he couldn't clean his own closet.

"Hard work is good for you," he said. "I work through the day. Your mother works at night. It's only fair that you share in the chores."

"We've always helped around the house," I told him.

"But we think you should help when we ask you to."

There was that "we" again. They were becoming a united front now.

I knew it was no good to argue with him, so I began to vacuum just to get it over with, going from room to room, grumbling all the while.

But my grumbling stopped when the vacuum cleaner bumped the lid off of an old shoe box in the bottom of his closet. I bent down to put the lid back on, and that's when some trinkets inside caught my attention. Black-and-white photos of my stepdad and his buddies in Vietnam. A letter from a soldier he had saved. And a Purple Heart. He had been shot in the leg while rescuing a comrade and hadn't even told us. And why would he? Why would he share something so special and intimate with three teenagers who gave him nothing but a bad attitude?

Hot tears stung my eyes and my heart ached. I began to see him in a different way. As a man. A soldier. A wonderful husband to my mother. And yes, I had to admit, a good father figure. A hero, even. My resentment turned to pride, respect, and admiration.

Wanting my brother and sister to know too, I called them into the room.

"Maybe we shouldn't be too hard on him," I said as we all looked at the Purple Heart.

My sister nodded. "I don't always agree with him, but he isn't a bad guy."

"He didn't even brag about it," my brother added.

Suddenly, it felt pretty good to be in a military family. To know that Mom was married to a humble man who had served and sacrificed for his country. To think that he cared enough for us to try to guide us with discipline. It made me grateful. And proud.

—*Tammy Ruggles*

A Sailor's Return

I waited until I was alone to open the package that had arrived from the Department of the Navy. Seeing the crisply folded national ensign lying on top, my throat tightened; vivid memories of Jacqueline Kennedy receiving her husband's flag at Arlington National Cemetery flashed before me. At that moment, I realized all those who serve our country, presidents and ordinary men alike, are equal at the moment of final rest.

Tucked under the flag I found a letter to my mother, some photographs, and three spent rifle cartridges.

The letter was from Captain M. D. Malone, Commanding Officer of the USS *Kansas City*. In accordance with my mother's request, the captain informed her, my father's cremated remains had been committed to the sea in full military burial. The ship, aboard whose decks the ceremony occurred, sailed from the Oakland Naval Supply Center in California, the very same port where, forty-nine years earlier, my father had boarded another ship, headed for the South Pacific, to serve his country in World War II.

During the war, we never knew the exact location of my father's ship, only that it was somewhere in the Pacific. At that time, posters tacked up on storefronts reinforced the need for secrecy, warning "A slip of the lip can sink a ship." Seven years old, I literally feared that the flaming battleship sinking into turbulent waves on the poster's background could be my father's.

Walking home from school, I would look at the little flags with gold stars in neighborhood windows and quicken my pace, hoping we would not have to replace our blue star with one of those. The day when the Kalish family around the block got word their son was killed, I remember agonizing whether someone had carelessly revealed the location of the battlefield in France where he was driving his Jeep.

On the best days, a letter from my father was waiting for me, proof he was still alive. A natural storyteller, his letters were wonderful, including countless tales of his shipmates, some poignant, some humorous.

I laughed at the story of a seaman leaning against the rail, so absorbed in staring down into the waves that he bent over too far and fell overboard. Scooped up and dripping wet, he suffered the hoots and jibes of his mates, who never let him forget.

Another night my father heard muffled crying from the bunk below his. Swinging down, he listened to an eighteen-year-old tell how he'd learned on the day he shipped out that he was adopted at birth. My father tried to assure the boy he would eventually come to terms with his adoption. The young sailor wiped his eyes with the back of his hand, "You don't understand, Barton. Being adopted doesn't make a difference. I love those folks so much; I just hope I get home in one piece so I can thank them for all they've done for me."

But the stories I loved best were of the kind and peaceful natives of the islands where my father was stationed. (We later learned these were the Admiralty Islands off the coast of New Guinea.) Page after page recounted evidence of their hospitality to the sailors who came into their small villages. Once my father mailed me a trinket handcrafted from tiny pods that one of the island women had taught him to make.

His letters were also filled with as many photographs as the wartime censor would allow. Smiling faces of strangers we would never meet fell out of the envelopes. Snapshots show my father holding dusky-skinned babies, clowning with older children and offering them chocolate, and embracing an elder. In some photos, the sweet and shy mothers of those babies are handing beautiful tropical shells to the American serviceman.

Some of those shells still sit on tables in our house. As my father grew older, he'd often pick up a pale and creamy conch and say wistfully, "When I die, I'd like my ashes scattered in the Pacific."

At the end of the war, as families happily awaited their veterans' return to peacetime, our street mirrored others across the country. Banners of "Welcome Home" festooned windows and doors. Neighbors gathered on porches and waved greetings the day my father, handsome and safe, sped up our front walk. New phrases cropped up in conversation: "lame duck," "Purple Heart," "missing in action."

My father's re-entry into civilian life included an almost daily recital of war experiences. His military rank was that of fireman, and he reliably performed the daily tasks given him by the Navy, involving the mechanical maintenance of shipboard equipment. He was an ordinary man doing what thousands did in that time of unparalleled patriotism. He won no medals for bravery; he did not (as I had so wildly imagined) torpedo enemy ships; he did not personally carry classified military information across enemy lines or perform uncommon deeds of derring-do. Most of his stories were about others and the observations he made.

Slowly, our lives returned to a semblance of normalcy, and these tales were taken down from the shelf less frequently. We put together a photo album of his "war days," and this, too, eventually found its way into an old dresser drawer. I grew up, and my father grew older.

The time came when one day my father had to fight a more personal battle, this one against Alzheimer's disease, where there was no possible hope of victory. Confounded by forgetfulness and telling stories that now had no endings, his erratic behavior transformed him into someone we barely knew. Most of the time, I had to remind him who I was. The painful decision was made to place him in a nursing home.

While helping my mother pack everything he would need for the rest of his life into two suitcases, I remembered how he loved to tell us about his tightly rolled sailor uniforms and how he managed to get all his worldly necessities into a compact and neatly packed duffel bag. I knew he would not have wanted to be packing for this trip.

My father never adjusted to the home. He appeared forlorn and alone, even though other residents surrounded him. His walk turned into a shuffle; his shirt came loose from trousers, which slid down over his hips as his appetite decreased. Our anguish increased as we tried in vain to make our visits with him meaningful. It was then I thought of the photo album of his days in the Pacific.

We sat on the edge of his bed as I slowly turned the pages. He pointed to the vigorous and tanned sailor with the blindingly white cap perched jauntily on his forehead.

"Dad, do you know who that is?" I held my breath as he stared intently at the picture.

"That's me!" For the first time in a long while a smile creased his face. He lifted the album closer to his face and began to mention names and places in disjointed sentences. It didn't matter; from some deep recess he was able to conjure up enough memory to temporarily revitalize him. No other diversions made him as happy as looking at the album.

One Sunday we took him to a mall where he halfheartedly waved at a toddler, whose mother did not encourage him to wave back. I thought of the island babies in the album and the parents who lovingly held them up to the healthy American sailor.

As his illness progressed, my father spent more and more time in bed, blankets pulled over his face. But if anything could capture his attention, it was the photographs.

One day after we closed the album, in a rare moment of lucidity, my father looked at me and said, "I'm dying. Please take me home. It's not good to die in a house of strangers."

I was overwhelmed with the enormity of not being able to grant so important a wish. But the family knew there was one thing we could do. We could help him return to the sea near the islands he loved so much.

We hoped our request to the U.S. Navy was feasible. Phone calls were made to federal offices, and wheels were set in motion. Within two days, with polite and caring military personnel smoothing every step of the way, we learned our government does work and that those who serve their country are not forgotten. We were informed that all sailors are entitled to full military burial on land or sea, at the government's expense. The communication read, "For years of service to his country, it is fitting that FN Philip Barton, USNR, be buried at sea from the deck of a proud vessel of the United States Navy." We even had our choice of ports from which his remains would sail.

The photographs sent by Captain Malone will be added to my father's album. They include a picture of seven young and able seamen firing a twenty-one-gun salute from the deck of the USS *Kansas City* as my father's ashes are committed to the sea. My brother, sister, and I each have a spent rifle cartridge.

The captain's letter to my mother ends: "The flag was flown at half-mast. The seas were calm and the setting serene. . . . It was our honor to have played a part in the closing chapters of your husband's life."

No greater hero could ask for more.

—*Edie Barton Scher*

Unspoken

I'm walking back to my office tent from the bathroom when I hear the crackle of static over the base's loudspeaker. I've grown accustomed to the sound in the six weeks I've been in Afghanistan. It usually announces severe weather, road closures due to mine-clearing activities, or gun ships getting target practice in a nearby field—the kind of information thousands of service members might need to know right away.

This time, however, the voice delivers an announcement I have not heard before. "Attention all personnel. A mass casualty incident has occurred."

I quicken my pace to a trot, and my tan boots splash dust puddles as I make my way along the gravelly path. As I near the office door, the speaker comes to life again, this time announcing a red alert.

"The base is under a direct attack," the voice tells us. "Don your Kevlar and body armor, and take cover in the nearest bunker."

I break into a sprint, shoving open the tent door and rushing to my desk. Staff Sergeant Kevin Tomlinson, the NCO who works for me, stands behind his desk, mouth agape. As an officer, I usually use a coaching style of leadership, but this is a time for direct orders.

"Get your stuff on and let's go!" I bark at him as I holster my sidearm and grab my body armor off the stand next to my desk. I swing my arms through it and bend under its weight. Adrenaline takes over, and I straighten up and grab my Kevlar helmet.

"Let's go!" I say again, grabbing Kevin's helmet and shoving it into his hands. I direct him to the rear exit of the tent and follow him out the door, struggling with my helmet's chin strap, which never buckles just right.

The bunker is not quite tall enough for us to stand up straight inside, so we stoop and duck-walk through the entrance. Benches line either side of the concrete tunnel. The snowmelt of early spring has left the inside of the bunker clammy, and I wish I had a jacket. Unlike the dry ground outside, the dirt inside remains saturated. Mud sucks at my feet. When I sit down, my knees almost brush against the person in the space across from me. With my helmet grazing the bunker ceiling and my boots sinking into the muck, I brace myself for an uncomfortable morning.

My concern about discomfort quickly passes. The loudspeaker announces again that the base is under attack. Questions flood my mind: *Are they re-announcing the first attack or announcing a new one? How many injuries does it take to cause a mass casualty announcement? Where are our attackers? Can I pull the trigger on my gun if it comes to that?*

News travels fast, even in a bunker. "There was a suicide bomber at the main gate," someone says. "It's because Cheney's here," someone else adds, referring to Vice President Cheney's "secret" visit to the base that had been widely broadcast on the news the day before.

I look across the bunker and see Master Sergeant Shawn Larson, wedged between two airmen I don't know. Shawn has been in Afghanistan for only a few days—the first combat assignment of his twenty-year career. His eyes scan the bunker, taking it all in. He sees me looking at him and shakes his head. "I don't know, Captain," he says. "This is gonna be a long six months."

I offer him a slight smile and nod. "Maybe for you," I say. "I'll be home in three months."

The loudspeaker announces "red alert" once more.

"How many of them are there?" asks an airman, maybe two years out of high school, with fear in her voice. "Why can't we stop them?"

A male airman farther down the bench gives a sarcastic reply that I don't hear because the "mass casualty" announcement sounds again. A few people laugh at what he said.

Master Sergeant Lee Spears, a hard-nosed Philadelphia native, hisses, "Did you hear that? Every time they make that announcement, it means at least eight people died. Eight of your brethren died, and you're making jokes?"

I'm not sure whether Sergeant Spears's information is correct, but I decide not to pursue the argument. Seriousness settles over the bunker. We sit in the quiet, listening for sounds of war.

Tension builds in the silence. I lean back against the concrete, not caring if my just-pressed uniform gets filthy. Closing my eyes, I think about my wife and infant son thousands of miles away. I pray we'll all make it out of this attack okay.

Half an hour later, the sky erupts in my ears as an F-15 Strike Eagle flies low overhead. A second one roars behind it, the deafening noise designed to scare the fight out of our enemies.

"Were those ours?" someone asks.

"They'd better be," the smart aleck airman retorts. "If the Taliban have started flying airplanes, we're in big trouble."

Everyone laughs, and together we savor the light-hearted moment.

We've been in the bunker for over two hours when the loudspeaker informs us we can return to our work centers. I go back to my desk and phone my commander's office to report that Sergeant Tomlinson and I are both back on duty.

Kevin's older than I am, but there is a certain childlike quality about him.

"You all right?" I ask.

"I'm fine," he says in a thin voice. He sits down at his computer, still wearing all his gear.

"You can take off your helmet and vest," I tell him.

He nods, but doesn't make a move.

Kevin is a reservist who usually works on a Ford assembly line in Detroit. He volunteered to come to Afghanistan because he thought he'd spend a few months handing out food and clothes to Afghans and playing with their children. Since arriving, we haven't been allowed to leave the base—it's been deemed too dangerous. Suicide bombings aren't part of his imagined deployment. He needs space. I leave

the tent and stand for a moment in the sunlight, letting the brightness recharge me.

I seek out a friend who works in the command
center. He confirms that the attack was a suicide
bombing at the base's gate. "Probably twenty people
were killed," he tells me. "Mostly Afghan civilians."

I return to my desk to see what, if anything, I
need to do as a result of the morning's events. I'm
saddened by the senselessness of it all. Across the
hall, another officer flips on the television.

"Hey," she says, "the bombing's on the news
already."

My heart sinks. I pound out an e-mail to my wife
to let her know I'm okay, and I hope that she'll see
the message as soon as she wakes up. I tell her I'll
call her the first chance I get.

That evening we talk, and I give her the basics
of what happened. For the first time in our marriage,
I feel like I can't tell her everything. I can't tell her I
was scared when the red alert sounded or that I felt
sick every time they called out a mass casualty. I can't
tell her that I didn't feel safe or that I prayed that she
and my son would be okay if anything happened to
me. All I can tell her is not to worry about me and
that I'll be home soon—the banality reserved for
distant acquaintances, not the intimate whispers of
best friends and life partners.

I realize she knows I'm holding back, but she doesn't probe any further. I love her even more for it. We hang up the phone, and I recognize that we both had our needs met—my need to protect her and her need to believe I'm safe. Still, I feel as though I've betrayed her, and I count it among the costs of war. This is the untold sacrifice of the military family: unspoken words, unexpressed feelings, unshared secrets.

Three months later, my wife and I embrace in the airport, our year-old son asleep on her shoulder. She is beautiful; he is pure joy. Later, we share a Pepsi, and I begin to recount my war stories, not holding back the details this time. I know she wishes I had shared all with her before, but she also understands why I could not.

She takes my hand and looks me in the eye, and I need say no more. Our friendship runs deeper than these secrets.

As I walk through the Baltimore airport in my desert camouflage, people stop me to thank me for what I've done. I smile and accept their kind words, knowing that they really belong to my wife. She is the true hero, a stronger soldier than I can ever be—keeping the home fires burning each day to give me hope for a brighter tomorrow.

—*Travis B. Tougaw*

Sisterhood of the Traveling Pans

Military spouses rely on each other. Some of us also rely on a good set of casserole pans—for as we move through this military life together, we can often be found toting piping-hot casseroles to friends we know well and to families we hardly know at all. Some people may say the casserole-bearing image of the military wife is an outdated stereotype. And maybe it is, for some. But time and time again, I have seen firsthand that the news of a new birth in the unit or a tragedy within a family down the street is cause for chicken breasts to be thawed and ovens to be heated to make a meal for a fellow military family.

My first experience with the sisterhood of the traveling pans was after the arrival of my first child. Exhausted by the birth and facing the unfamiliar rigors of parenthood, my husband and I could not focus on putting together dinner. Fortunately, we did not have to think about meals. The morning after my son was born, the sisterhood went into action. A steady stream of dinners arrived, and casserole pans were loaded into our refrigerator. The first wave of meals included a big dish of baked ziti and a huge salad, a chicken-and-vegetable casserole, and a turkey pot pie. To this day, I remember the dishes that people made; they tasted delicious after a long day of being a new mommy and showed how much our fellow military families cared about us.

Sadly, my most recent experience with the sisterhood of the traveling pans was with the loss of a family's four-month-old baby to SIDS. Across the world in Iraq, my husband was delivering unthinkable news to his soldier; back home, the sisterhood was working to help his family. While the much-needed details were handled, hot food was also delivered to feed the people who came to mourn with the family. It was a small gesture by many women who cooked their gifts with heartfelt sympathy.

Not only does the sisterhood turn out for big life events, we also like to cook for our many social gatherings. If you don't have a good collection of appetizer recipes (or places to buy appetizers) at the beginning of your marriage to a soldier, you most certainly will have one before long. Putting on a good spread for an event or celebration is not as important as having a good time, but knowing how to make a mean dish of bacon-wrapped shrimp is definitely a plus. A good recipe for dip has been known to be passed far and wide within sisterhood circles—from home to home and post to post.

And a military spouse knows just when to share a good recipe or a comforting casserole or a kind word.

I learned this when we received one of our first invitations to a social. Of all places, we were invited to my husband's brigade commander's house. Being a young wife who was new to the Army, the prospect of making a dessert to bring to this important event was daunting. It was not the time for trying something new, but I whipped out my casserole pan and mixed together an untested recipe for apple caramel bars. I should have known better; fifteen minutes before we were going to leave, I was pulling gooey squares out of the pan and trying to arrange them into something that resembled a dessert.

Upon arrival, I put my dish on the table in the beautiful dining room next to much better-looking desserts. I tried to slink away before anyone noticed; however, the brigade commander's wife stepped in my way and thanked me for bringing something. I must have looked embarrassed because she asked me if something was wrong. I blurted out how I had tried really hard to make something special and how the recipe had failed miserably, and I did not have time to make something else. She smiled at me and picked up one of the bars.

"They look fine to me," she said, taking a big bite. "And they taste good, too."

The sisterhood of the traveling pans understands what it's like being a new military spouse; the sisters have been in your shoes before.

When our husbands deploy, we could just slide the pans to the back of the cabinet. Instead, we try hard to keep them handy. While our husbands are away, the sisterhood gets together for dinners to recreate a family atmosphere. Out comes the recipe for the beef casserole we ate over at someone else's house the month before or for the tuna casserole found in a magazine. Sharing meals and time together helps us to relax at the end of the day, and it sure beats the macaroni and cheese we were planning to make for the kids or the back-up trip through the drive-through when we just don't feel like cooking.

Often, the member of the sisterhood phoning to invite you over for breakfast or showing up on your doorstep with a casserole in her hands is a good friend. At the same time, it is not unusual for someone you hardly know to bring a meal to your door or to call with a dinner invitation. Over the course of our many moves, I have made meals for families I knew only by name as well as for those I knew well. Usually, I serve or bring my famous baked ziti—the same dish someone brought to my house when I had my first baby. Both close friends and casual acquaintances within the sisterhood have responded in kind, inviting me to dine at their homes or bringing a covered dish to mine.

We sisters of the traveling pans share a common goal: to support one another, in good times and in bad. And sometimes support means just sharing a home-cooked meal together.

Unfortunately, the times I remember most clearly are when the pans came out for the days that were loaded down with bad news. When I lost a pregnancy, I wasn't sure I wanted to see anyone. The thought of food was far from my mind, yet the pans filled with delicious food still appeared, delivered by my friends who also served up the warmth of their love and the comfort of their words.

Then there are those nights when you drag yourself home from work, too tired to think, much less prepare a meal, and a sister friend will hear your exhaustion over the phone. The next thing you know, she's standing in your kitchen, dishing out just the nourishment that your body, and your spirit, needs. Some nights the pans stay packed, and we head out with another military spouse to kids-eat-free night at a local restaurant.

The sisterhood of the traveling pans has probably always existed in the military, even though the natures of the women, their gatherings, and the food have probably changed over the years, at least somewhat. It is also true that food does not cure all our woes—like husbands deployed to far-away places, the dishwasher that breaks two days into a field-training exercise, kids having trouble adjusting. But doing normal things, like sharing a meal, with someone who understands helps to soothe the soul. That's what it's all about, really, providing nourishment and companionship when our sister military spouses need it most.

—*Janine Boldrin*

In Sunshine and in Shadow

Nell would never forget that morning. It had started out as a typical warm summer day. In sync with the splish-splash rhythm of Nell's gentle pulls, Guernie chewed on her timothy hay while Nell hummed.

Nell had planned a full day of chores. After milking Guernie, she would churn the milk to get cream, chop wood, and weed the garden. And as soon as the kids got off the school bus that afternoon, all of them would get busy picking green beans and snapping them for canning. Her youngest child still had hands small enough to pack the snapped beans into Mason jars. Her oldest had just gone off to Vietnam, leaving his young wife and young son in their care. It had been tough to let him go, but everyone knew there was no way for him to make a living on their small farm. The Army would give him training, maybe pay for a college education.

Nell didn't want to think about the odds of her son coming back alive from Vietnam. The community's losses had been high in both World War I and World War II. Her father had died in World War I. One in four of the valley's sons had not come back from World War II. The only living reminder of World War I was her great Uncle Mack Culpepper who, fifty years later, was still taking his silent walks up and down the valley road.

When her Will had returned from World War II, Nell had been grateful. They got married the day he came home, just as they'd planned. She had prayed for his safe return, and now she was praying again, this time for their son's survival in Vietnam. She had counted the months until Will came home by putting a notch beside his name on a support beam in her family's barn. Now, she was doing the same for their son, Will Jr.

Nell had just poured her pail into the milk can and settled down for a refill when she felt the rising sun warm her back. She felt good. She amused herself by watching her shadow cast onto Guernie's glossy brown side. Maybe, she thought, the sun was shining on her son today, too. Several wrens were darting back and forth gathering hayseed dropped by Guernie. The barn cat was not even bothering the birds, content to lap up the milk Nell had given it.

Nell was taking it all in—the smell of warm milk, fresh hay, the chatter of birds, the peaceful farm animals, the warm sun on her back—when she heard a footstep behind her. She felt a chill. Someone or something was behind her. She was about to turn around when she froze with fear; her image on Guernie's side had been overshadowed by that of a huge man with a raised hand.

Guernie jolted. Nell, motionless, tried to calm herself, noting the shadow was not moving closer. But the stare at her back was running shivers down it. She was in a vulnerable position. She had to do something. She tried to continue pulling milk, but Guernie would not cooperate, swatting her tail furiously.

"Stop it, Guernie," Nell said. "There are no flies in here." She was glad to hear her own voice calming Guernie . . . and maybe whoever was behind her.

Still frozen in the depth of the shadowy figure, Nell now saw that the raised hand was not moving and the person was not coming closer. She started singing "You Are My Sunshine" to buy time, keeping rhythm with her feet to see if they would work.

Nell usually did the milking in the shed. It was large and open on one end. She would tie Guernie along the back wall, where the cow could easily drink water out of a trough and eat hay out of the back of an old seeder box on the planter in the shed.

She told her husband that Guernie seemed to enjoy the sounds and smells of the fresh outdoors as much as she did. The anxious cow often led Nell out of the stable to her milking site.

But now Nell thought, If I'd milked Guernie in the barn, I would not have my back to whoever is behind me. I would have seen whoever is coming. I could have gone out the other door. Just as Nell began the second stanza, she saw the shadow move forward. But she was ready; she had gripped the milk bucket firmly. She turned quickly and had the pail ready to throw when she saw the shadow was her great uncle, Mack. Nell gasped. She swallowed hard.

"Hello, Mack," she said as serenely as she could. She took another breath and added, "Nice day."

Despite all the rumors and speculation, Nell believed he had never hurt anyone. Yet his imposing frame; dark, vacant eyes; and stone-cold silence alarmed most everyone. Mack had not spoken to anyone since he got back from the war in November of 1918. He seemed oblivious to everyone and everything.

Nell remembered well the stories about the day Mack went to war and the day he came back. His whole family, including her mother, had been at the station when he got off the train.

Then, as now, Mack was a big man—more than six feet tall with the broad shoulders and the large

arm and leg bones that visually identified generations of the Culpepper family around the county. He
looked pretty much the same as he had when he'd
left. He had lost weight, but so had most of the other
servicemen who'd come back.

The high school band was there to welcome all
the survivors, everyone in a festive mood. But Mack
did not flash his big grin or let loose with the hearty
laugh that he'd left them with four years earlier. He did
not run up to join his relatives rushing toward him.
He did not greet and embrace them, as they so longed
to embrace him. He just stood there with hollow eyes
that seemed to look through and beyond them.

Nell's mother told her how quiet it was when
they took him home. They did not take him to the
victory celebration. They could not get him to talk.
He didn't show any recognition of his baby picture
or the photo of him graduating from high school.
Standing in the back row where they put the tall
boys, he was still taller than the others. A newspaper
article describing his going off to war with other valley boys didn't interest him at all. He just let it lie on
the table. He stared blankly at it, just as he did the
newspapers they later put in front of him, trying to
interest him in at least reading.

Wherever they led him, he would just stand or
sit if there was a chair, without doing or saying any-

thing. His father and brothers even took him to the corn fields and handed him a hoe to see if he would chop out the weeds like they were doing. He just stood there.

When his family built a new house in town, Mack Culpepper was left in his ancestral home, which his family had rented to farm tenants. The tenants earned extra money to look after Mack. They tried to get him to break his routine of only coming out of the attic to eat when the bell rang, to go to the bathroom, or to take an afternoon walk after lunch.

One caretaker family, who had three sons killed in the same war and another who committed suicide, was the most sympathetic. They quickly proclaimed him to be a victim of shell-shock and taught their kids not to fear him.

Another caretaker family decided he was just lazy. They made it clear that, if they would've had the money, they sure wouldn't be working six days a week, ten hours a day, for his family, who they proclaimed were living in town because the country was not good enough for them. They reckoned Mack was actually the smartest one in the valley because he knew how to get out of hoeing corn.

A health-care worker who had trained with the WPA after the Depression said Mack could be a victim of what a lot of World War I veterans suffered but nobody talked about: venereal disease. She did not appreciate it when Mack's resentful caretaker joked that in high school all the ladies had chased after Mack and probably French women were no different, that maybe Mack had been caught by loose women in France.

The valley people never accepted Mack's daily walks down the road. They were afraid of his silence, and he became inhuman to many. Kids accepted dares to go near him. Others taunted him. But Mack paid no attention and never stopped taking his walk, not even on the day the body of a man whom everyone felt had killed his wife and molested his own children was found alongside that very road. He had been strangled by barbed wire from a nearby fence.

The investigating sheriff's brother had also been a survivor of World War I. The sheriff knew about the pitiful attempts of soldiers trying to protect themselves in their foxholes behind barbed wire fences. Soldiers were shot and left to die hanging in the fences. The sheriff had a copy of Robert Service's poem about it, called "On the Wire." He wondered about Mack. As the sheriff and coroner were removing the body from the ditch by the road, Mack had walked by. Looking up, the sheriff could have sworn that Mack saluted him, but he could not be sure. Mack continued on, not breaking his slow, steady pace. The sheriff, knowing the history of the victim, decided this was a case best left unsolved.

As time went on and more people forgot about the old wars, things got worse for Mack. His health was failing and his walks got shorter. He would often be seen resting by the road, just staring out into the cattle fields. According to the teacher who had once taught at the one-room country schoolhouse but who now taught at the school in town where all the kids were bussed, as soon as the word "pervert" came into the valley vocabulary, Mack was labeled with it. Despite the teacher's best efforts to teach the students about war casualties, Mack was the object of ridicule. Some of the younger generations of his family even started to call names and throw stones at him. But not Nell. She still remembered her mother's stories.

And at this moment the past was very much alive for her.

Mack didn't react when Nell quickly choked back her gasp, smiled, and dropped the bucket. She instantly knew why he had his hand up. He was pointing into his mouth, which was opened wide. Somehow, Mack apparently knew that his niece, Nell, sometimes filled in for her aunt, who was a dental assistant in town. Nell looked to where he was pointing and could see that he had tried to pull his own tooth. It had broken off and was badly infected.

Sensing Nell's relief, Guernie relaxed and resumed eating. The milking would wait. Nell pointed to the truck, and she and Mack left for the dentist's office.

After that, the skies were a little bluer for Mack. The taunting stopped. He was human after all, the people in the valley said. He had a toothache.

That night, Nell cried before setting out to the barn to put another notch in the beam for her son. Her two-year-old grandson wanted to help. Nell brushed his hair out of his eyes as she lifted him up. He was so carefree now. And his father was still alive in Vietnam. She managed a smile. And began to sing softly, ". . . Please don't take my sunshine away."

—Mary Kuykendall-Weber

Please Tie Your Shoes

Raising a son is not for the light of heart. Danger lurks everywhere. When my son was growing up, it was my job to keep him safe. Sometimes that meant supervising him closely. Sometimes it meant restricting his activities. I tried not to be a "smother mother," but sometimes—okay, a lot of times—I'd warn him to "tie your shoes so you won't fall and break your neck" . . . or to "not run with that stick or you'll poke out an eye" . . . or to "look both ways before you cross the street or you'll get run over by a car."

Truth be told, I never stopped feeling like it was my job to keep him safe. Even today, I can't seem to help but express my concern when he's facing some grown-up situation that could cause him discomfort or difficulty, if not harm.

"I know, Mom, tie my shoes or I'll fall and poke out an eye," Nick kids me.

And I smile at this little joke between us. But my fear has always been genuine.

In September of 2006, my fear multiplied, gripping me so tightly I couldn't breathe. My son, my only child—the artist, the reader, the charmer, the comic, the well-trained rifleman—had been sent to Iraq in his third year of active duty to the United States Marine Corps.

My world turned upside down. Many nights I would lie in bed with a band of pain pressing across my chest and think I might not make it through this night or this week or this month or this year. I wasn't afraid of my dying. Indeed, in my mind, that was my only choice if, God forbid, anything happened to my son and he died before me. I figured I'd be right behind him; that my heart would just stop.

The weeks leading up to the day he deployed were horrible. Every rational fear was magnified a million times by what I didn't know and, more important, by what I did know. Having been a peripheral part of the Marine Corps community for nearly three years, I knew one thing: Any mother's son can die. I think most of us military parents go through the numbers game and the endless questions in our heads. *When was the last time someone in my family died? Are we due? When was the last time I prayed? Did God hear me? Will my daughter-in-law be able to call me if the worst happens, or will she be so devastated that she curls up in a ball and I won't know for hours?*

My thoughts were always wandering to the dark places. I felt melodramatic one minute and practical the next. My son was my first and last thought every day. I struggled through conversations with God. Not wanting to appear that I was asking anything for myself, even though I was, I prayed for all our troops and their families. Sometimes I would think, *Maybe God plays no part in this at all.* I hoped, though, and prayed that he would protect my son and keep him safe so I could see his face, hear his voice, and feel his wonderful bear hugs again.

I foolishly signed up for online news alerts, including the Department of Defense's casualty releases. One after another would pop into my email. "The Department of Defense announced today the death of a Marine who was supporting Operation Iraqi Freedom . . ." Day after day they came, until I could no longer bear to read the names of someone's son or husband or father and my head hurt just looking at the first few words.

Nick was able to call me from Iraq on a few occasions. He always assured me he would be fine, and I wanted to believe him. I wanted to tell him he'd better be, but I chose my words carefully every time we spoke, just in case it would be the last.

I asked him once about a unit that had suffered many losses and if he thought it was a leadership problem.

"No," he said. "Sometimes, Mom, it's just crap luck."

That wasn't what I wanted to hear.

When my son left for recruit training, I was grief-stricken the whole thirteen weeks, and when my friends compared his time at boot camp to their kids going away to college, I truly wanted to rip their heads off their shoulders. I kept thinking that perhaps the grief I felt was a premonition.

Halfway through his deployment, we received word that the unit would be extended from seven months to an additional 60 to 120 days to accommodate the surge of American troops. In my mind, if not in reality, the longer he was there, the greater the risk of injury or death. My sense of powerlessness was overwhelming. The sleepless nights became incessant, the one-ton elephant on my chest became a two-ton Humvee, and I became even more obsessive about sending him care packages filled with home-baked cookies and baby wipes.

My daughter-in-law and I talked on the phone three or four times a day. Our love for Nick was the common denominator that allowed us to support one another so completely. We held each other up on days I know neither one of us could lift a feather, so weak were we with fear.

During the deployment, my son periodically had access to the Internet. His communications with me during those times were what sustained me the rest of the time. We chatted about anything but his job. The house, cooking, crazy animal antics, and furniture moving mishaps were safe topics. I would go back to those instant messages, which I learned to save, and read them days later, looking for hints of despair or signs of stress. I saw only my own.

Thankfully, time did not stand still. On May 5, 2007, my son and a couple hundred brothers from Kilo Company, Third Battalion, Fourth Marines stepped off the white buses that transported them from the airfield to the base in California. His bride found him in that crowd of hundreds and ran into his arms. I waited my turn, gladly. My anticipation of seeing him was not unlike the day he was born. I hugged him as hard and long as I could without looking like a mom over the edge. My eyes watered, but I didn't sob, pass out, or wail like I thought I might. I think I was too relieved, too grateful. My faith in God restored, I was humbled in the presence of those boys turned men, and all I could do was hand out homemade cookies and hug every Marine I had worried about and prayed for throughout their deployment. I'm a lucky mom, and I thank God every day.

The interesting thing is that the fear has not passed. Nick has been home for more than seven months, and I still can't shake the fear. He has no visible scars, and only he knows if his soul was wounded. I keep looking into his face, searching for answers, but all I see is my baby boy all grown up and somehow still the same.

I told my son to expect me to keep worrying for a while. I'll continue to tell him to be careful driving, skateboarding, swimming, walking, and breathing. He understands, I think, when I just have to say, "Tie your shoes, son, so you don't trip and break your neck. Okay?"

—*Katie Wigington*

A Leatherneck Legacy

In the sweltering hot August of 1943, in a world filled with messages of war, a young man of twenty-one years stepped off a cattle train filled to the brim with scared and eager young men. Most of them had never been this far south or met the dreaded sand flea that calls this place home. The place was Parris Island, South Carolina, a small marsh island surrounded by mud and water.

In August of 1993, a similar event occurred when a young man of eighteen years stepped off an air-conditioned bus and double-timed to line up on a set of yellow footprints painted on the asphalt. The other young men crowding the bus were also scared and eager. Although more of them were well traveled than their counterparts of 1943, few knew of the sand flea. This was still Parris Island, South Carolina, the training ground for the United States Marine Corps, but much had changed in fifty years.

When I entered the Marine Corps in 1993, I was not only privileged to serve my nation in the best fighting force in the world, I also was able to enter training fifty years to the month after my grandfather. Henry Powers served in the Fourth Marine Division during World War II. He participated in the island-hopping campaigns of the Pacific Ocean and fought on Iwo Jima, Saipan, Tarawa, and Roi Namur. Fifty years later, I served in the Fourth Marine Division in Charleston, South Carolina.

When my grandfather visited for my graduation, I gave him a tour of the base and training facilities. He pointed out familiar areas and also quite a few unfamiliar ones. Of course, the barracks and other buildings hadn't existed when he'd trained. He slept in tents and dined in the same. I slept in an air-conditioned and heated barracks. Much of the swamp where he and his fellow recruits waded through chest deep mud is off-limits for training now, useful for nothing but scenery.

One adage that all old-time Marines tell the younger ones is, "It was much harder when I was in." As the younger Marine in this case, I like to think that it was just different, but that's only because it makes me feel more manly. The treatment of the recruits is much different these days, and many people would consider it to be much softer. I tend to agree. My three months at Parris Island were much easier than my grandfather's were. There were times I wished the drill instructors would be harder and meaner. Now I look at Marines currently in the Corps and tell them it was harder a decade ago when I went through. Even the hand-to-hand fighting training has been changed because of one or two injuries over the years. I thought that was the point. Our DI promised us a call home if our boxing opponent had to be carried from the ring. I never got to make that call home, but at least neither did my opponent.

After he finished his time at Parris Island, my grandfather and the other newly minted Marines made their way to Camp Geiger for infantry school. There, they stayed in Quonset huts. Amazingly enough, fifty years later, I stayed in the same ancient huts for Marine combat training. A few improvements had been made since my grandfather's training there. Although there was no air conditioning, we did have heat, which was a special comfort for the rare weekends we weren't in the field. My grandfather spoke of wood stoves and extra layers of clothes to satisfy his heating needs.

It was here that I departed from my grandfather's legacy; rather than becoming a Forward Artillery

Observer, I received more training. I transited a short piece down the road to Courthouse Bay for landing support school. Even though I varied from my grandfather's cycle, I never strayed far from the family legacy. My uncle, Tony Peters, had been an instructor at the same combat engineer school during the Vietnam War twenty-five years earlier. Many of his stomping grounds were relatively unchanged; I learned in the same classrooms in which he once held lectures.

After I'd completed all my training and reported to my Marine reserve unit in Charleston, South Carolina, I once again joined the legacy left for me by Henry Powers. As a reservist, I was privileged to join the same division that my grandfather had fought in. Even though a reservist, I was tremendously honored to be a part of The Fourth, even if it wasn't "The Fighting Fourth" of World War II fame.

As I look back and think of the stories my grandfather told me of hand-to-hand combat and of storming beachfronts, I know that it was he who convinced me to join the Corps. I was influenced not only by his glory days in the Marines, but also by the person he became because of the Marines. I wanted to be that kind of person. Aside from the unique honor of becoming one of the few, I was allowed to share a special privilege and to celebrate the anniversaries of my grandfather's service while crawling through the same mud and shooting on the same firing ranges. I joined the military and the Marines, specifically, because of his legacy. That alone brought us closer, but I think it was his visit to my graduation ceremony at Parris Island that brought us closest. We shared special memories that few grandfathers have with their children's children. All too often grandchildren lose touch with the older generations that contributed to their upbringing in so many ways. I didn't. I shared a bond with my grandfather through our shared experiences, one of which began with this question, "So how many times did you get caught swatting sand fleas?"

—David W. Powers

This story was first published in The Fighting Fourth, *1st quarter 2006, a newsletter of the Fourth Marine Division. It has been edited for publication in this book.*

Memoir of an Army Girlfriend

We don't wear medals or combat boots. We're not always first in line to be notified if the uniformed man who stole our heart has been hurt or killed. We stand by our men with no guarantees, no spousal assistance, and no documented existence of a relationship between us and the one we love. We are Army girlfriends.

Many servicemen (and women) go overseas without rings on their fingers but with love in their hearts. They depend on the promises and memories they've made, and they hope for the best with no assurance that the significant other they leave behind will still be there when they return. My boyfriend, Mike, is one of those soldiers.

In August 2006, Mike, a front-line infantryman in the U.S. Army, left for a fifteen-month tour in Iraq. Some military couples choose to exchange vows in a justice-of-the-peace ceremony prior to deployment to ensure stability and benefits during and after the deployment. But Mike and I felt it would be better in the long run to let his deployment test the strength of our relationship and the strength within ourselves. We had no idea what we were getting ourselves into, but we were up for the challenge. Little did we know that challenge could not even begin to describe the world that awaited us.

For the first two months he was gone, Mike and I had no contact. I wrote him letters every day and waited by the phone for his call. Finally, in October, the call came. Tears flooded my eyes, my heart pounded against my chest, and my voice shook with elation, fear, excitement, and worry as I struggled to utter out a garbled, "I love you." Though we could speak only briefly, I could hear in his voice that he was more scared than I was—not about the danger of his surroundings, but rather for me. Mike was well aware of how emotional I could be but had never heard me break down like I did then. My throat clenched, my breath caught in my throat, and all I could say was, "I love you, I miss you," over and over between quick, ragged breaths.

I have always been known as the "tough girl." Nobody could break my spirit or push me past my emotional limits. When Mike left, all that changed.

My life suddenly went from constantly socializing and going out with friends to staying at home alone surrounded by every picture, movie ticket stub, dinner receipt, and memento of my faraway love I could find. Instead of partying with pals on Friday nights, I was gluing heart decals around the edges of paper memories, capturing the simple joys we'd shared before he left. Making those reminders of my love and sending them across the ocean kept me sane.

Enduring a deployment tests the strength not only of the men and women fighting for our country but of those who are left behind. For a long time I struggled with this newfound vulnerability. I had never felt so helpless in my life and was disappointed in my inability to control my frequent fits of hysterical crying. My pillowcases became so saturated with pools of cried-off mascara that to this day black streaks still run down the middle of them.

I would be lying if I said it got easier. It never does. You hope it will, and then you learn that you're just postponing another emotional meltdown. There were, however, some positive outcomes to the heartbreak I endured while Mike was gone. When he came home, words cannot describe how I felt. Not only did I feel the anticipated wave of relief, but I also felt a sense of stability that I hadn't expected. I looked into my boyfriend's eyes and saw a different man. He wasn't just the young guy from Texas who had stolen my heart with his camouflage pants and Southern drawl. He was a warrior. A savior. A hero. My hero.

I, too, had changed. I was still the emotional girl I had been fifteen months before, but I had a new sense of confidence . . . in myself as well in my relationship with Mike. We had some rough patches during the deployment. At one point we even decided to end things. I thought that maybe if I didn't think about him, I would be able to deal with the distance better, but I soon found out I was completely wrong. Looking back, the separation did nothing but give us faith in the future.

You see, we military girlfriends face a burden the wives do not: uncertainty. Sure, everyone is uncertain whether their boyfriend, fiancée, or husband will come home. But for us, that is not the only worry. For us, there is also the risk of our men deciding while they are away that the distance didn't affect them as much as they'd thought it would. Perhaps they'll come back to the States wanting to be unattached, wanting nothing to "hold them down." It's much easier to walk away from a girlfriend than it is to leave a wife.

After you've come through such a long, treacherous, draining, and ultimately life-changing experience with your boyfriend, nothing can stop you.

Come hell or high water, you two know that you can achieve anything as long as you are together. Though it will bring out the worst of you—tears, anger, resentment, fear, sadness—a deployment can also bring out the best in both of you.

I won't say it's easy, because it's not. I won't say I didn't cry myself to sleep or invest in a body pillow to pretend he was there with me every night. I did those things. I also cried, screamed, and tore my hair out, among other coping mechanisms. But now I have the man of my dreams home with me, and it is clear skies and an open road ahead. Once you get through a deployment, you learn two things: There's no turning back, and there's nothing you can't overcome.

—Sarah Casey

The Price of Freedom

I watched as a car pulled into the driveway and stopped. Seated on my couch, I could see some type of military insignia on the side of the door but couldn't make out what it was. As I leaned forward to get a better look, two uniformed men stepped out of the car, and my heart froze.

The day our son Josh came to my husband and me and said, "I signed up for the Marine Corps," I was not worried. Several months later, at my son's graduation from boot camp, surrounded by good-looking men in uniform, my young daughter came to me with stars in her eyes and said, "I want to marry a Marine." Again, I was not worried.

We were a Corps family. Our military roots reached back through the years to another place and time. My father enlisted in the United States Marine Corps at the tender age of seventeen. Nearly three years later, he stood in black ash at the base of Mount Suribachi, on the island of Iwo Jima, and helped to bury 1,900 Marines as the American flag whipped in the breeze above him. His two younger brothers followed in his footsteps and became leathernecks. On different turfs, both boys fought the North Koreans, the younger of them at the Battle of Chosin Reservoir.

Military was in our blood. As a young boy, my son could be found weekends dressed in camouflage, filling his backpack with MREs, and disappearing into the woods behind our house to camp out. Ever precocious, he eventually grew out of his military phase, and upon entering middle school, he took to donning a suit and tie and carrying a briefcase. Still, it was no great surprise when in his senior year he broke the news that, on his own, without our consult, he had signed on with the United States Marine Corps. And I was not concerned. But that was before September 11, 2001.

Nine-eleven brought a whole new scenario to my mind. We had been attacked on our own soil. There were rumors we would go to war. And I wondered what this would mean for our men in uniform, especially our Joshua. I thought about my brother, a soldier during the Vietnam War. An only son, he'd remained stationed in Arlington, Virginia. He never saw action. But somehow I knew Josh would. Still, because he had joined the Marine Corps as a reservist and was part of a truck unit, we hoped he would be among the last to be deployed. We were wrong.

On March 20, 2003, Josh was part of a military-led convoy moving out of Kuwait and into Iraq. For the next several weeks, my husband and I stayed glued to the television set. We kept it on, though muted, while we slept. We weren't afraid, just apprehensive of what would happen, and we felt a need to keep abreast of the news. But this would be a different kind of coverage. No one had ever watched a war unfold on television before, and my son was there in the midst of it, right on the front lines of battle. I searched every face on the screen, hoping to see his.

While we, like every other military family, wrote letters to Josh and prepared packages to send into the field, my son, halfway across the world, watched the statue of Saddam Hussein topple and smiled for a photograph in the former dictator's dining room in Tikrit. Each day, I kept in contact with his girlfriend, a sweet pretty young thing from the Czech Republic. We encouraged each other through e-mails and made very long-distance phone calls when the news would not wait. I garnered camaraderie from other Marine mothers and wept in empathy for the families of each reported casualty. But I was a woman of faith, and I always believed my child would come home. And in the spring, my son was returned to me.

For a while, life reverted back to normal. My youngest daughter had met and married her Marine, and they began their life together, stationed in North Carolina. When the next official phone call arrived, it was for two of my loved ones. First, my son-in-law, Earl, deployed for Ramadi, and my daughter and her new baby made the temporary move back home. Then, in November 2004, Josh found himself officially part of India Company and on his way to clean out insurgent-infested Fallujah. Josh and Earl, sent to different areas of Iraq, were always on the lookout for each other, hoping for an encounter with a touch of home. Then finally it happened. They found themselves face to face, for a few moments, just enough time for a bear hug and a quick news exchange. They would not meet again in Iraq.

By the time of that second deployment, we were familiar with the routine. Josh had been returned to me once; now we hoped and prayed for his safe return again. As with the first deployment, I believed our son would come home to us, and I was not seriously concerned . . . until today.

This day, I watched through my living room window as an official car pulled into our driveway. Two uniformed men got out, and my heart nearly came to a stop.

I knew the procedure. They come to your door, two men in uniform. I had thought about it, run the gauntlet in my head several times. I was ready, as much as I thought I could be. But now I was paralyzed with fear; my chest beat a deafening cadence as the scenario unfolded before me.

The men walked around to the back of the car and conversed together. Then they opened the trunk, removed something, and in a few moments slipped back into the car and drove off.

For a time I couldn't move. My heart refused to calm itself. It was still retreating from fear of the one thing we hoped and prayed would not happen.

The next month my son came home. Earl followed shortly thereafter. Both have now left the military and gone on with their lives. Earl and Jill have another child. Josh is finishing college. I was blessed to have my children come home to me.

I've always been a cheerleader for the cause of those who sacrifice to protect our liberty and all that it stands for. But that day in my living room, I gained a new appreciation for our men and women in uniform and the families of these men and women who pay the ultimate price for our freedom. Freedom to pursue the life we love, freedom that extends to us all, freedom I will never take for granted again.

—*K. R. Fieser*

Her Heart Is Red, White, and Blue

When I got off the phone with Jennifer, I was very upset. We'd always been close, and the distance I now felt between us hurt and concerned me. I love all three of my children dearly and equally, but for some reason, Jen and I had always shared a special bond. Now that she was an adult, we were not only mother and daughter but also close friends and confidantes to one another . . . until she and her family had moved to Japan. I tried to keep the connection strong with frequent e-mails, letters, and phone calls, but Jen had grown increasingly more aloof. She was just not the open, caring daughter I knew.

I'd been barely twenty when Jen arrived, only a year after her brother, my firstborn, and I felt somewhat overwhelmed with being a new wife with two babies. As she grew up, Jen became my helper and then my buddy. Later, she also became my port in the storm during the dark years when I had panic attacks. Jen always knew how to soothe me, what to say and do to calm my fears. Many times she held me when I cried, listened to my problems, and was just plain caring.

Now she was a woman with her own family. Over the last eighteen years, I have watched my daughter transform from a demure teenage girl into a strong woman, loving mother, and devoted military wife. As they've moved from place to place, it is Jennifer who has made each temporary house a stable home.

When her husband, Ed, was transferred to Japan three years ago, for the first time in her role as a Navy wife, Jennifer was thrown into an environment that was completely foreign to her. She had to set up house in a place where she did not know the language or the customs. She had to learn to drive on the opposite side of the street, how to convert the dollar into yen, how to take the bullet train to Tokyo, and much more. While Ed was out to sea, she had to be both mom and dad to their children and to literally keep the home fires burning, just as she had when they'd been based in the States.

Yet, despite all her responsibilities and hardships—no matter how far she'd lived away from us before—Jen has always been warm and open with me. Now I wondered if our last three years apart had weakened the bond between us.

She'd been so logical and unemotional; it seemed she had turned a deaf ear to my concerns. Where was the daughter I remembered? Where was the caring, compassionate person? I admit my problems at work weren't as drastic as her move to Japan, but I really wanted to hear her opinion. Instead, she'd brushed them off. I made a mental note to talk to Jen about our phone conversation the next time I saw her.

About a month later, my husband and I went to Japan to visit Jen and our two grandchildren. Ed wasn't there because he was on a tour of duty with Operation Enduring Freedom. One afternoon, my husband took the kids and dog to the park, so Jen and I settled in for what we do best—sit in front of a fire, sip tea, and chat.

"Jen, I want to talk about something that's bothering me."

"What, Mom?"

"Well, I'm going to get right to the point. I'm concerned because you haven't seemed like yourself for a while. You've always been so loving and caring. Lately, when we have a conversation, you seem cold and logical. Don't you feel things like you used to?"

There, I'd said it. I held my breath. I'd been pretty blunt.

Jen got a faraway look in her eyes, glistening with tears.

"Mom, I know you have problems in your life, and I don't mean to minimize your feelings. You know I'd never deliberately hurt you. It's just, well, I feel everything too deeply. I have to steel myself from being too vulnerable.

"You don't know what it's like to be a military wife. To go to bed alone every night wondering if your husband will come home. Do you know how much it bothers me to see my children growing up without their dad? Do you know how much it hurts to see people being disrespectful to the country my husband is trying to protect? I cry alone some nights. I question if I am making the right decisions for the kids' future. Am I helping Payton choose the right college? Am I giving Emily the guidance she needs to grow up to be a decent young lady? I worry about all these things."

I listened raptly, in awe of my daughter's responsibilities as well as her devotion, compassion, and strength.

"If I didn't rely on my faith in God and know he is in charge, I couldn't do it," she went on. I talk to him every night. I used to wonder sometimes if he heard me, but looking back, I know he did. It just didn't seem like it at the time."

One nation under God, I thought. And I felt proud that my daughter clearly emulated this principle every day of her life. Jen and the kids attend church regularly, but I'll bet her best prayers are the ones she says alone in her room each night.

"People don't understand how much we sacrifice as a family," Jen went on. "I'm not complaining. I am so proud to be a Navy wife. I just wish other people understood what we give up. That's why the flag flies day and night on our front porch—to remind others how great our country is because of our guys who make the big sacrifices. I promised myself I'd do my share by keeping things going at home until Ed gets home."

Now I understood. It wasn't just the guys making the sacrifices. Entire families, especially the wives, shared the burden—bravely and proudly. Hot tears ran down my cheeks as I reached over and hugged my daughter, who sobbed in my arms. I felt badly for her, and yet I knew that with her faith and strength to guide her, she would do fine.

Jen hadn't stopped caring. She cares deeply . . . about her husband, her children, her country, and me. How could I have doubted her? My daughter is as compassionate as ever—in fact, she's even more so than ever, because now her heart is red, white, and blue.

—*Sallie A. Rodman*

Wings to Fly, Arms to Hold Me

When the innocent question "Where are you from?" pops up at a cocktail party or over lunch with a new coworker, most people have the mystical ability to toss out a place name and voila! Instant conversation. Not me. I stumble and stutter, fishing for the right response.

Growing up in a military family has turned explaining where I'm from into a strategic endeavor. If I answer with where I was born, they'll expect me to have some familiarity with the place—and I don't. We left before I was a year old. I could just pick one of the many places I've lived at random—but where shall I identify with today? Ohio? Texas? California? West Germany? Sometimes I can come back with a cheery, "We traveled a lot," or "We were a military family," and that does the job. But I usually feel a need to explain myself, add extra detail. It's that extra detail that leaves me stammering.

Once I get rolling with the detailed explanation, I don't want to leave anything out. My short answer turns into a monologue. If I am diverted, by my short attention span or by somebody quick on her verbal feet, I cast about for a way to return to the original topic. The mission must be completed. But even I am not immune to the blur of inattention that crosses a person's face when he really didn't want ten minutes of exposition in reply to a four-word question.

Maybe the reason I want so badly to explain is because, for me, life was two-dimensional until we finally landed, and stayed, in Alaska. It's not that life was boring or devoid of meaningful experience before then. Instead, I simply hadn't acquired—a different experience that would enable me to put what I'd already lived into perspective. I needed to know what it was like to stay in one place long enough to build lifelong friendships, to talk about how a place has changed over the last ten years. It's taken me nearly twenty years in Alaska to feel like I finally have a home. Now that I know what it feels like to put down roots, I can more fully appreciate what came before.

Some of the details of my early life have blurred in the fog of distance, time, and recollection. It's a bit like looking through a fish-eye lens. The immediate object of my focus comes up nice and clear, but the rest tends to fade away as first one and then another memory comes trundling into my mind and then falls into the void of present day.

I remember getting on and off planes, convinced the jetway was a dragon waiting to eat me, and running after airplanes in the airport because we didn't leave ourselves enough layover time. Is it self-pity that makes it seem as though I, the smallest, had to tow the largest suitcase?

I had friends that were good but never "best," because we just didn't have enough time together for our friendship to reach that elevated status. The relatives I knew changed immensely between sightings, because we met up only once a year, if that.

By the time we hit Alaska, I was a seasoned pro at packing and unpacking. Traveling every two or three years as a child taught me what it was to be an American in another country where some people liked you a lot—and others disliked you. A lot. We were stationed in what was then West Germany during the height of the anti-American protests in the 1980s. I remember being puzzled when we returned to the United States. Schoolchildren here don't do bomb evacuation drills? No armed guards on the school bus? It speaks well of my parents that I never realized that my overseas upbringing was unusual until I encountered its U.S. counterpart at eight years of age.

When we made it back from overseas, I was also shocked by the sheer volume of consumer material here in the States. It was bewildering to see an entire aisle full of different shapes, sizes, and brands of cereal boxes—not to mention the immense selection of clothing. Gone were the days of picking from a single round rack of my size; now I had rows and rows of them to choose from! I'm not so sure this is a good thing. How many times have I found myself in the cereal aisle, wondering if we really need this many kinds of Cheerios?

I am thankful for an upbringing that, instead of telling me about differences, showed me the differences and let me feel what they were, like a blind woman tracing the lines of a child's face. Because of the way I grew up, I know very well that our way is not the only way. More important, I know that it is not the best by default. I can allow myself to question, to wonder, and to see different people as revelations instead of threats. This, in turn, enables me to appreciate what is good about life here.

It was hard not to have solid soil to put roots in. Once I'd grown up and moved out on my own, I transplanted myself from apartment to apartment every two or three years because it just didn't seem right to stay in one place for too long. Mobility was, to me, the breath of freedom; I couldn't imagine anything worse than being trapped in one place. It wasn't until recently, approaching the completion of my second decade in the same city, that I finally realized that stability can be good and that stability and freedom need not be mutually exclusive.

People who have spent their entire childhood in one place have an entirely different portfolio of experiences than I do, and it is fascinating to compare notes. I wish I could have had their stability and closeness, their familiarity with family and friends; they wish they could have experienced some of what I have witnessed. Yes, traveling was an adventure, but so is exploring the home front; I feel doubly blessed to have had the opportunity to do both.

So I've finally learned how to respond to that tricky question, "Where are you from?" Instead of saying where I was born or where I have been, I answer with where I am. "Alaska is home," I say. But the twinkle in my eye must give me away; I've got more of a story to tell than that. "But I grew up in a military family . . ."

—*Lisa M. Maloney*

The Fabric of a
Seasoned Navy Wife

I was twenty-four years old and didn't know the first thing about the military or about being a Navy wife. I was from Kansas, far from the world of warships, military agendas, and ship deployments. However, all that changed in the summer of 1986.

A year earlier, my husband Greg had abandoned our marriage, leaving me no option but to press on alone. We lived in Wichita, Kansas, at the time but hadn't been there long enough to make new friends. As each month passed, I grew desperately lonely. I yearned to live closer to my family. So, after much prayer and thought, I decided to start over in California, where my dad and stepmother lived.

One July morning, just after my divorce became final, I loaded up a small U-Haul trailer with the remnants of my former life. By late afternoon, I was making my way across the flat landscape of western

Kansas. As I watched the sun set on the horizon, my thoughts turned to what the future might hold for me.

Within a week of my arrival, I was offered a job as an administrative assistant at a cruise travel agency in the San Francisco Bay area. Immediately, I befriended one of my coworkers, Valerie. She was a Navy wife with two small children. That summer, my friendship with Valerie grew. On the weekends that her husband was underway with his ship, Valerie invited me over. We exchanged stories about our lives. She shared the hardships and sacrifices as well as the pride she and her family experienced through supporting her husband's military career. Her faith and strength inspired me, and our friendship was like healing salve to my heart. I thanked God for bringing her into my life. For the first time since my husband had left, I felt the dark pit of loneliness lifting.

Then one summer day Valerie invited me over for a casual barbecue. Her husband Mark had invited one of his Navy buddies, a young and single petty officer named Ray. Mark and Ray worked together in the engineering department on board the same ship.

"So where are you from?" Ray asked me as he handed me a glass of iced tea.

"Kansas," I answered, trying to hide my nervousness.

Suddenly, his face lit up. "That's interesting," he said, with a chuckle. "Did Valerie tell you that Mark and I are stationed on the USS *Kansas City?*"

"Yes, she did," I answered.

An awkward silence suddenly fell upon us. I took another sip of tea and adjusted myself in my chair.

"Where in Kansas did you move from?" he asked, piercing the silence.

"Wichita," I quickly replied, hoping my pat answer would suffice to answer his questioning. I wasn't ready to talk about the life I'd left behind.

To my surprise, another grin flashed across his face. "Really?" he said, this time with a certain inflection in his voice that now piqued my interest.

"What's so amusing about that?" I asked.

"The USS *Wichita* is the sister ship to the USS *Kansas City*, and it's moored right behind our ship."

Odd, I thought, and I would have dismissed these coincidences as just that—except for one last question he asked that convinced me our blind date was more than just a coincidence.

"Were you born in Wichita?"

"No, I was born in Lawrence, which is up in the northeastern part of the state."

At that point, his grin had turned into a full-blown Cheshire cat smile. Now I was chuckling too.

"What is it this time?" I begged to know.

"Lawrence is my middle name!" Ray exclaimed.

Over the next several months, whenever the USS *Kansas City* was in port, Ray and I were together. He was self-controlled and far more mature than his twenty-one years would suggest. Remarkably, his positive disposition and self-confidence didn't come across as boastful. Most wonderful of all, he made me laugh, something I hadn't been able to do for a long time.

At times, though, I wondered whether dating a sailor was wise. Everything about it seemed wrong, but it felt so right. His demeanor proved his integrity. Gradually, I was able to entrust more and more of my heart to him. On his duty days, I visited him on board ship, bringing a plate of his favorite cookies. Those shipboard visits were a constant reminder of the privilege it was to be allowed on a warship and to see the in-port operations of the ship as well as Ray's life up close. Although this lifestyle was nothing I had every known before, I embraced it. My former life in Kansas now seemed another world away.

Then, one evening as I was making dinner, Ray came to me with a look of concern on his face. "My ship is due to go on a deployment soon," he said.

My heart sank when I heard the word deployment. I knew what that meant, thanks to my friend, Valerie. "When do you leave?" I asked, contemplating the looming separation.

"May."

My mind began to race. *Would our relationship survive the long separation? When he returned, would we be able to pick up where we left off? Or would time and distance change everything?*

"You know," he began to explain, "deployments are hard on relationships." My heart skipped a beat at the serious tone in his voice; I sensed more to come. "Even though we just met this summer, I hope you will still be here when I get back. You have no idea what a difference that makes way out there in the middle of the ocean."

There it was. He wanted to know if I'd be here for him for the long haul. I knew in my heart I would be. I realized getting through my first deployment wouldn't be easy, but I believed in us and felt confident I could embrace this lifestyle. That evening I gave Ray my verbal commitment. Then, just before Christmas, he proposed. I accepted, and the following spring we were married. A month later he left on deployment.

As the years passed, people commented on my status as a Navy wife. I heard comments ranging from, "I don't know how you deal with all the separation. You must be very strong," to "I didn't get married to sleep alone." On many occasions these comments prompted me to wonder what it is that makes an ordinary woman like me into a seasoned Navy wife. After all, I was no different from any other woman. I didn't possess any special capabilities or insights; I just lived under a different set of circumstances.

Then one day it came to me. While hemming my husband's new dungarees, it occurred to me that a Navy wife is much like two types of material: denim and spandex. Like denim, I had a tough inner resolve to support my husband. The inherent pride of having a husband in uniform fueled my energy and determination to go the extra mile. And like spandex, I became flexible when I needed to protect that inner resolve with an optimistic attitude. As a result, I became more content in my role as a Navy wife. However, these strengths didn't happen overnight. Instead, I was more like a woven cloth, a slow transformation in which the two types of fabrics blended together to produce a compatible partner for my husband. Gradually, I learned to yield in loving compliance; then I was able to stretch in ways I never thought I could.

One winter while Ray was on his third ship's deployment, my kids and I awoke late one morning to discover we had no electricity in the house due to an overnight windstorm. Suddenly, I realized my car was in the garage and that with no power my garage door opener wouldn't operate, leaving me unable to get to work. The situation was further complicated by the fact that the evening before I had thought-lessly hit the garage door button to bring the door down for the night, not realizing I hadn't pulled my car far enough inside for the door to clear the back end of my car. I hadn't noticed that the garage door stopped short of the trunk.

First, I tried to manually lift the garage door, but it wouldn't budge. It seemed locked in place. I contem-plated my dilemma. Should I trouble my neighbor this early in the morning before he headed off to work, or would that be imposing on his busy morning sched-ule? Embarrassed, I dialed his number and explained the pickle I was in. Moments later he was over study-ing the problem. He grabbed my husband's ladder and climbed up to the garage door opener on the ceiling.

Fortunately, he knew about the emergency pull-cord that operated the door manually. However, the trick was in knowing how to release the ten-sion on the door mechanism so it wouldn't spring loose and cause the door to come crashing down. I braced myself for that possibility as my neighbor gingerly unhooked the spring. Instantly, the mecha-nism popped under the pressure. Cringing under the weight of the old wooden door, I couldn't hold it up but for a brief second. The door jutted out of my grip downward in one quick and forceful thud onto the trunk of my car. My neighbor scrambled down the ladder. We girded ourselves up underneath the bottom panel and together carefully rolled it back up the track. To my surprise, my car was unscathed.

Being independent didn't mean that I would never need help from others. Instead, I discovered the real meaning of being independent: knowing when to reach out for help. My initial dose of independence was a springboard for me, but there were other obstacles for which more stamina and more stretching was required. Just when I thought I was all tapped out, Uncle Sam would require a smidgen more.

With each deployment, measurable amounts of growth occurred, compounding my confidence level for the next deployment just around the corner. Like denim, I became frayed at times, but never completely undone. I learned to stretch and flex, like spandex.

In 2003, after serving twenty-one years, Ray retired from the U.S. Navy. I, too, retired, although unofficially.

While waiting to get my new retired status dependent's identification card in the PSD (Personnel Support Detachment) office at Naval Station Everett, in Everett, Washington, my thoughts took me back to the day when I became a dependent of a larger family called the United States Armed Forces. On the day I married, Uncle Sam became my boss, too. I quickly realized that he was domineering and expected much. My first glimpse of his uncompromising nature came when we had to change our wedding date three times before we had a date in which Ray and the USS *Kansas City* wouldn't be underway. As frustrating as it was, that was the start of my understanding of the scope and the importance of the ship's mission.

Despite the challenges of the military lifestyle, there were benefits that were equally important and rewarding. Joyous homecoming celebrations gave my kids and me a sense of accomplishment. I looked at them as my reward for a job well done, since I had my own mission to fulfill at home with our two children. My husband knew I was confidently handling the issues on the home front so he could carry out his part in the ship's mission without preoccupation or concern.

Today, we work side by side in our own business, and we still use the same basic principles of denim and spandex. I believe those principles have contributed to the success of our joint post-Navy journey in life, just as I know the qualities of strength and flexibility created the resilient fabric of this military wife.

—*Lisa A. Phillips*

Alone in a Crowd

Today, while my husband was busy, I took my camera and drove to Blue Hills Reservation. Just south of Boston, this reserve with miles of hiking trails makes a nice Saturday afternoon jaunt. The beautiful weather drew crowds: families, couples holding hands, friends young and old, and the occasional loner like myself.

I don't mind being alone; I rather like it. I people-watch and I listen, speculating on the lives of those around me, sometimes correctly and sometimes not. Sometimes I start up a conversation with those who are willing.

I decided to climb Great Blue, a hill well under 1,000 feet but high enough to have a weather observatory on its summit and a ski slope perfect for beginners. I chose the red trail: rockier, steeper, and more of a challenge than the green one. Weaving through the other hikers, I moved ahead at my own pace.

Around a curve, I stopped and waited while a woman kneeling in the trail took a picture of her three boys. I noted her patience as she tried to get them all to look at the camera at the same time. I wondered where her husband was and thought he must be just ahead. Often the men move quickly with a toddler on their shoulders while the mothers herd the other siblings at a slower pace.

Later, I saw the woman at the summit and then at the observatory, where she was again squatting in front of the boys with the camera to her eye. That she was clearly taking great care to capture each moment impressed me.

One of the boys made rabbit ears behind his brother. "Oh, Tommy has such a nice smile. Why don't you smile, too," she urged him. Agreeably, he dropped his hand and smiled.

"So handsome," she said.

Again, I admired her calm and her patience with the boy's puppy-dog antics.

I remembered how hard it was to get a picture of my three without the rabbit ears or without one of them crossing his eyes and sticking out his tongue while the other two looked angelic.

Later still, I stood behind her as she listened to one of the boys read information about the weather station. She gave him all her attention. Catching me watching, she smiled.

"What grade is he in?" I asked. He looked too young to read such big words.

"Second," she said. "He's a good reader."

Then the rest of the story came out.

One of the boys is her son; the other two are her neighbor's. Their father is in Iraq. So is her husband. The pictures she's taking so diligently will be e-mailed to the men, a poignant reminder that life continues without them, that the boys are growing and miss their daddies.

It was her day to take the boys. She and her friend take turns planning activities for the trio on the long, lonely weekends—to give each other a breather and to give the boys companionship with a friend who also misses his dad. Her friend would do the same for her another day.

Then, while the boys scampered on the granite outcroppings, she shared her struggles, her loneliness, and her fears. She seemed glad to talk, seemed to need to talk. I was happy to listen.

I didn't do what I wanted to do, which was to give her a hug. It is not my hug she longs for, and I was hesitant to move into her carefully guarded emotion. As she spoke, I felt tears form; her eyes remained dry. She's trained herself to control her feelings, just as the military has trained her husband to do the same.

Though I had spent the day by myself, I had done so by choice and went home to my husband, a man who had served in Vietnam forty years ago, a man who has sealed off the ugly experience of combat from me. When his memories surface, he faces them alone. So then, despite his presence, I am alone even while at his side.

This woman, by herself in a different way and certainly not by choice, would be alone until, if all goes as she prays it will, her husband returns. Then, because this is what war does to its combatants, her husband will lock away the moments he spent in Iraq, and she will feel like she is alone, even when he is beside her. But she'll learn that he is with her even in his silence. She'll come to understand that for him silence is peace, and this is a gift she will gratefully give—her silence and understanding—along with her love.

—*Ruth Douillette*

Sentimental Journey

The lyrics of that sentimental song poured monotonously from the sound system of the ship as if to remind us all of why we were aboard. I needed no reminder. It had been nineteen months since I had seen Charley.

The year was 1951, and we were finally on our way to Japan—Mark, almost three, Jordan, fourteen months old, and I, a young military wife, uncertain about the future, making this trip to bring our family together. For me, the past two years had run the gamut from exciting and romantic to difficult and lonely.

It had been an idyllic life in 1948 and 1949 on the Army post at Fort Belvoir, Virginia, a beautiful and historic area. My husband and I were among friends, deeply in love, and starting a family with the birth of our son, Mark. The scuttlebutt about overseas assignments had diminished, and we decided the time was right to give Mark a little sister. Shortly after my pregnancy was confirmed, Charley returned home from the post very late one day. Without a word, he went straight to Mark's room and bent over the crib. When I entered the room, he pulled a paper from his pocket and handed it to me. He had been ordered to Japan.

Families were not allowed to accompany the servicemen, but the Army promised we could follow later. I would spend the intervening time in Indiana near our parents.

On the day of Charley's departure, we spent the last few minutes walking in the park, just the three of us, like any ordinary family on a sunny April afternoon. Then we got back in the car, and Charley insisted that I drive to the bus station, let him out, and keep driving. He didn't want any further goodbyes. I did just that. I didn't see him board the bus that took him away.

My expected travel orders did not arrive in June. Instead, the Korean War escalated and dependents were not allowed to make the trip. My sorrow was amplified when my father was killed in an accident. I struggled to keep a positive attitude during this painful period. In September 1950, our daughter, Jordan, was born.

Jordan was thirteen months old when documents finally arrived giving us permission to travel to Japan. After a train ride to Seattle, we spent Thanksgiving Day in port with hundreds of other anxious wives and bewildered children. The next day, a mixture of rain and snow buffeted the ship as we boarded. A howling wind tried to dissuade us from the journey, but the USS *General McNair* sailed.

Children vomited and mothers cleaned up as we passed a "bug" around for the first three or four days. The laundry room, hot and steamy, was the center of activity. Heavy fire doors posed an extreme danger for small children, so my children and I spent most of our time in the sparsely furnished cabin we shared with another Army wife and her two teenage daughters. Six bunk beds lined the walls, and a large, open, tiled floor provided a play area for the children. We played with plastic horses and cowboys and small cars that raced from one end of the room to the other with each list of the ship. The music played continuously from morning until bedtime, interrupted only by announcements.

"Beep, beep. Beep, beep." The piercing sound of the signal for lifeboat drill jarred the children awake from their naps. A uniformed seaman directed us to a ladder leading to our assigned lifeboat.

"I'm supposed to climb that?" I questioned, holding Jordan, clad in snowsuit and life jacket, against my own bulky coat and life jacket.

"Yes, ma'am," he replied with authority.

Leaning against the side rail, still weak from the flu, I inched my way up the ladder. With help from the seaman, Mark followed behind on all fours. Luckily, it was only a drill. Fear of my inability to maneuver a lifeboat had there been a real emergency and the reality of the dangers to my children overwhelmed me. After the drill, I welcomed the security of the cabin. Our performance gradually improved as this exercise was repeated a dozen times during the trip.

On the thirteenth day, one of the teenagers yelled excitedly as she peered out the porthole, "Look, everybody! I see something. We're there! Mom, we're there. Come and see!"

Her excitement spread through the cabin, and we crowded around the small round window. The coast of Japan was within sight. Arriving in early evening after the port had closed, we were required to drop anchor in the bay and wait until morning to dock. The lights on the shore were visible through the porthole. Our husbands were there, waiting. "Please, God, give me patience," I prayed.

The ship was alive with activity in the morning. Ironically, it was December 7, 1951. On that very day ten years earlier, I'd listened to radio news reports of the bombing of Pearl Harbor by the Japanese. When President Roosevelt declared the "Day of Infamy" and announced we were at war, fear and sadness filled my heart, as it did for most other Americans.

Now, here we were, coming to this country that had once been our enemy.

During the docking procedure we were allowed on deck. Hundreds of uniformed servicemen, flowers in hand, stood on the upper level of a building on shore. We each strained to find a familiar face. Hearts pounding with anticipation, we rushed back to the cabins and waited . . . and waited.

The major, whose family shared our cabin, came first. "Daddy! Daddy!" the girls screamed in unison, leaping into his arms and smothering him with kisses. Their mother stood back, face wet with tears. He hugged his daughters, burying his face in their hair, and then reached out to his wife. The family circle was complete.

Several minutes passed as I listened to excited greetings in the hallway. Then came the sound of more footsteps. They paused at the door. My heart thumped in my chest. Then a familiar, handsome, suntanned face appeared. His shoulders were broader than I remembered, his smile brighter. The worry, anticipation, and the drills were gone. The sentimental journey was over. My love was in the room, and I was in his arms at last.

—*Lou Hamm*

Now I Know

For most of my life, the military existed for me only in abstraction. It was something that was discussed in the news or romanticized in the movies, but it wasn't anything real to me . . . until I met Jed.

I had been coaxed out for a night on the town with a few of my girlfriends. It was Labor Day Weekend 2001. I was shaking it with gusto when Jed crossed the dance floor and took my heart by storm. It was love at first sight. The angels were singing. The light from the disco ball seemed to focus just on him. I think I must have had hearts shooting out of my eyes.

As he passed, I smiled in an attempt to make a connection before he disappeared again, perhaps forever. He seemed surprised to be noticed, which I thought amazing, since he was by far the best-looking person in the club, maybe the whole galaxy! We exchanged a few words, and then he was gone.

Later I noticed him standing nearby with friends. Truth be known, when we finally talked it was boring, and I was about to say goodbye when something clicked. He suddenly brightened up, gently grasped my arm, and said with a big smile, "Oh, you're smart. Let me buy you a drink." We talked nonstop from that point on, until the club closed and my girlfriends dragged me away, leaving both Jed and me with a desire to see each other again.

Shortly after that first meeting, Jed went away for the weekend. He called one night and told me he was concerned that I would have a hard time being with him because of his job. He worried that I would end the relationship once I found out more about the military lifestyle. This was a big issue for him. Since I didn't really know what he was talking about, I just brushed it off. How bad could it be?

Two days after our conversation, eager with anticipation for his return, I walked into work and saw the devastating images of the crashing towers in New York City and the wreckage at the Pentagon. Jed was mid-air, and I knew he'd be near both Washington, D.C., and New York City during his return flights. I was on pins and needles until I heard from him.

He was fine, just shaken, having learned of friends who had not survived the attacks. He spoke with a kind of urgency that I had never heard before when he told me he had to sew new patches on his uniform before work and that he would be busy for a while. For the first time, I understood that maybe his job wasn't like everyone else's.

A year after meeting, we were engaged. It all happened faster than I could have imagined, but we knew that we had found the right fit in one another. Time seemed to stop when he got down on his knees with the most beautiful proposal I'd ever heard. For weeks thereafter, I would get distracted by the gleaming diamonds on my ring finger. Could this be real? It was. Wow.

Upon getting engaged, we learned that Jed would be transferred to San Diego, California. I had always wanted to move to California, but as we began organizing for the move we started to get concerned about practical things. For instance, because I was Jed's fiancée and not his wife, we would have to pay separately for my household goods. I would not have insurance. I would not be allowed on base when we arrived in San Diego, which was an issue because we would have only one car. I would not be privy to any information regarding Jed if he was to be injured. And the list went on.

I had never dreamed I would be planning a wedding based on practicality, but we decided to elope and to have a larger ceremony sometime in the future. Life has an interesting way of throwing curve balls. Again, there seemed to be more to this military thing than I had thought.

We attended a friend's wedding in Lake Tahoe and got married ourselves in Reno before flying back to New York. What a stark contrast. The wedding we'd attended in Tahoe was an extravagant affair, dripping with flowers, loaded with food, guests, and music. Ours in Reno involved an empty wedding chapel, a single iris wrapped in a silk ribbon, Jed, the priest, and me. By the end of the service, however, we were all in tears, including the priest. It was a tender and loving ceremony stripped of all drama, pomp, and circumstance. It was not the fairy-tale wedding I had imagined, but it was intimate and genuine. If Jed had not been in the military, we never would have had this experience, which turned out to be both a blessing and an honor.

Originally we thought we would keep the marriage a secret. Well, needless to say, our vows were not a secret for long. We were happy and eager to share our joy.

After driving our car, two dogs, and houseplants across the country, we found a great little bungalow for rent just a few blocks from the beach, cliffs, and sub base at Point Loma. It was an ideal location. Our new life as a married couple had begun.

So there I was, newly married, in a brand-new place and learning the ropes of being a military spouse. There was even a class I could take to indoctrinate me into the ins and outs of my new situation. It was a bit of an adjustment, and at first, I wondered what kind of alternate universe I had entered.

Just as things seemed to get into a rhythm, Jed was deployed. It was my first deployment, and I didn't know what to expect. It was a strange, lonely, and often heartbreaking time. We would go weeks at a stretch without talking, and when we did talk it made the distance seem that much greater.

During the long stretches of silence, my imagination would run wild and it would terrify me. I tried not to think about the awful things that could be happening to my husband, who knows where, but with all of the war news circulating it was difficult to keep my mind on other things. Before he left I made him a care box that included, among other things, a picture album and a couple of music mixes. At least by listening to the songs I had put in the mixes, I felt closer to him somehow.

While in San Diego we received orders to Honolulu's Pearl Harbor in Hawaii. What an adventure. In Honolulu, we lived in Navy housing, right across from the Navy-Marine Golf Course and within walking distance of the mega NEX, commissary, and Pearl Harbor base. It was like living in a kind of resort community, complete with member ID card.

When people came to visit, they reminded me of how many things in my life were different from the "civilian" way, but I had become so entrenched in the jargon, behaviors, ideas, and traditions of the military lifestyle that I didn't see it anymore.

In Hawaii, there was never a shortage of things to occupy our time. Some people complained of "getting off the rock," but we enjoyed every last bit of it. Being in Hawaii with so many other Navy personnel helped to ease the shock of deployments and the strain of Jed's long hours. It was a kind of community that I hadn't known before.

While we were in Hawaii, we blossomed as a couple and learned to support each other on many different levels. Jed went through dive school and the Sailor of the Year process, where he was named Sub-Pac Sailor of the Year and Runner-Up for Pacific Fleet Sailor of the Year. Dive school made him face a number of physical fears and pushed him to physical limits that he had never dreamed of. I would hear him doing breath holds in the tub and worry that he wasn't coming back up for air! The Sailor of the Year competition pushed him to a whole different set of limits. He was proud to represent the United States Navy through his abilities and integrity. For me, it was an opportunity to provide support and encouragement. We both were excited that in addition to furthering his career, the experience had strengthened our bond.

It was during this time that we also had a large renewal-of-vows ceremony back in New York. After a couple of years had gone by, we considered forgoing it altogether, but in the end, we both agreed it was a meaningful way to bring our families and friends together through our union. It turned out to be an amazing ceremony with music, singing, and loving words. Later, the food, company, and dancing kept us all together until well after midnight. We were blessed yet again.

After only six years of service, Jed made Chief. I was proud of Jed's accomplishments before and after his command issued me my very own primer on how to be a good Chief's spouse. By then, I had figured out a thing or two about being a Navy wife and fully understood the bumper sticker, "Navy Wife: Hardest Job in The Navy."

When Jed made Chief, we knew he would be deployed again soon. We were told he would meet his new boat in Japan sometime in November. Well, one Wednesday afternoon in October, he received a call at work. His new boat had stopped in Hawaii briefly en route to Japan and invited him over to their temporary mooring. He went. The next day he received another call. This time they informed him that they might want him to go with them to Japan that weekend. On Friday night the call came at home, informing us that Jed would be leaving with the boat the following day for six months, after which he would be returning not to Hawaii but to San Diego. Guess who got to arrange another move?

Well, all worked out just fine, despite the mad scramble and goodbyes. Despite the sleepless nights, the worry, the phone cards and letters, the moving around and the smell of submarine that just won't wash out of anything, we have managed to find the silver lining—the laughter and the fun in our lives. We have learned that time spent together is precious and creates the memories that get us through the times when we are apart.

I didn't know anything about the military before I met my husband. I just thought it was about guns and war and killing and ugliness. Now I know it is about community and fellowship, pride and integrity, and doing one's duty for our country. It is about serving for the safety and freedom of everyone who lives within our borders as well as for many who live outside of them. I have learned about dedication, discipline, perseverance, and bravery. I have met many men and women who work tirelessly to uphold this country's honor and to support the people who miss and mourn them from afar.

To my husband and all of the other men and women who serve our country: I once was ignorant of your sacrifice, but now I know and I salute you!

—*Rebecca Jayne Boswell*

Farewell at Gate Nine

I sat in an empty row at gate nine of the Burlington, Vermont, airport. Early for my flight home, I tried to read my book, *The Confessions of Saint Augustine*. Swirling dust motes suspended in a ray of sunlight from a nearby window kept lulling me in and out of consciousness. I had just spoken on my cell to Sarah and Hannah, my daughters, ages thirteen and eleven. Ten days of separation had been too long. I smiled to think of how I would sneak into their darkened rooms later and run my fingers through their silken chestnut hair as my lips found their foreheads, whispering into their dreams. Hannah, half asleep, would wrap her arms around me and say, "I'm glad you're home." Sarah, adolescent even in slumber, would mumble and turn away. But even that would be enough for me.

Three families drifted into the gate area. One sat to my left, another to my right, and the other across the aisle. Many more followed. I was only slightly aware that they were connected in some way—maybe a tour or a family gathering. Around me, the families spoke about incidental things to one another. "Did you see that fumble?" "It cost them the playoffs." "Who made the cookies?" "Kim. She knows you like them." "I'm bringing a picture phone." "I didn't have time to get one."

The boys in these families, some thirty in all, were mostly about twenty years old, with closely shaven heads and smooth skin. Dressed casually, they had fully loaded backpacks and duffle bags at their feet. Some were tall and slender, others short and stocky; some were fair-skinned, others dark. One boy had his arm around a young woman.

The woman to my right took a family photograph for the people across the aisle. At the click of the shutter, the split second that would etch the memory forever, each family member placed a hand on the young, clean-shaven boy sitting in the center, like the laying of hands or an ordination.

At the row's end, another young man, maybe in his thirties, sat next to his wife and two little girls. One of his daughters, perhaps about five, cried unabashedly. He wrapped his arms around her as she buried her head in his chest. The wife looked away.

Shortly, ten or twelve older men arrived, dressed in crisp camouflage Army fatigues with shiny black boots. Arms free, carrying no bags, they were not going, I reasoned. Clearly, they were there on official business. Their statures were commanding, yet gentle, like seasoned veterans who had walked the front line of human endurance. Their names were embroidered on their shirts, to the left, above a pocket: Noyes, Mosler, Cadieux, Callahan, Hester, Morris, Nichols.

Once in the gate area, they separated themselves, ceremonially approaching individual families. The boys stood beside their mothers, fathers, sisters, brothers, wives, girlfriends. Introductions were made, hands were shaken, and nice words were exchanged. Occasionally, someone laughed, but it was a restrained, nervous laugh, a polite gesture.

Next to me, Lieutenant Noyes stood erect in front of the family with the woman who had taken the picture. Looking at Noyes from the side, I could see behind his glasses. Deep crow's feet outlined his soft eyes. "He's a fine young man," he said to the mother about her son. "Don't worry about him. And thank you." But she couldn't offer a reply to this. I wondered why he'd thanked her. Was it for raising him to be a fine young man? For allowing him to go to war? I tried to return to Augustine's leap of faith.

The other uniformed captains and lieutenants went from family to family, offering measured words of reassurance that sounded like condolences. I was an uneasy voyeur, surrounded by my subjects, an intruder in the most intimate of moments.

During a group picture, all the boys gathered by the window of gate nine, where the snow-covered Green Mountains filled the background. One of the older uniformed soldiers stood quietly next to me, observing the scene with a laser-beam stare. He was tall, with black hair and deep, almond-shaped, brown eyes. His badge read "Cadieux."

"Excuse me, sir. Do you mind if I ask what's going on here? My name is Stephanie. I'm a writer."

"Sure," he said softly. "I'm Captain Cadieux. These boys are with the Third 172nd Mountain Infantry. They're the last of my unit to be sent off."

How little has changed, I thought. More than 200 years ago, Ethan Allen led his Green Mountain Boys over these Vermont hills into the American Revolution. I wondered if any of them were the ancestors of these boys.

"Where are they going?"

"Ramadi, Iraq, in two weeks. Right now, they're going to Fort Dix, where they'll be suited up and given their gear. We had a total of 165, but these are the last thirty to go. They're all volunteers." He paused. "We've already lost three."

"I'm sorry." At a loss, I asked, "Have you been?"

"Yes, I just spent six months there." His eyes deepened even more. He bore excessive knowledge of what these boys would see.

"How long have you had them in your charge?"

"Two years."

I thought about how long their families had had them.

"What'll they be doing there?" I asked.

"Mostly patrol. We train them in things like hand-to-hand combat, marksmanship, land navigation, riot control, and minor life-saving techniques." He pointed to one boy who was sitting across from me. "He's a medic."

"Why Ramadi?" I asked.

"It's where they're needed. Ramadi's the toughest place right now."

"And what will you do after they leave?"

"I'll be working on casualty assistance," he said softly, looking down at his feet. "We do a great job training our men, but we're not so good at helping them return or at helping the families when they don't. It's important."

The gate agent began to announce the initial boarding of our New Jersey–bound flight. The little girl with the pigtails began crying even louder. The conversations subsided as the boys embraced their families, girlfriends, and wives, one by one. The boys began to pick up their duffle bags and backpacks.

"Don't worry, Mom," said the medic. The sound of his mother's muffled sob broke through the silence. The medic, head down, used his index finger to get a foreign object out of his eye as he walked down the jetway single-file among the others. Captain Cadieux and the other officers stood to the side, hands folded behind them, thin-lipped and sober, a soldier's farewell.

My husband met my flight at the airport just before midnight. During the drive home, he asked about my trip. I told him bits and pieces about my planned thesis on *The Confessions of Saint Augustine*. But the scene at gate nine hung in my mind . . . and still does, like the backdrop of one of my stories. Only I can't write the ending. And perhaps I never will.

After arriving home and just before going to bed, I walked into Sarah and Hannah's rooms, lingering after each kiss, suspended between joy and sorrow.

—*Stephanie Cassatly*

Do What You Have to Do

The weak afternoon light filtered in through the living room window of our house in Germany. The girls were home from school, my husband had come home early from work, and dinner was bubbling away in the Crock-Pot on the counter in the kitchen. I had been relaxing on the couch for a few minutes when my husband, still dressed in his BDUs, purposefully stepped into the room.

"Hey," he said as casually as he could, "I'm going to Kuwait in three days, and I don't know when I'll be back."

What? Did I hear that right? Can the Army do that to us? It was November 2002, a little more than a year after the September 11 terrorist attacks on the United States. So, it looked like our government was going to . . . do what? Retaliate? We had heard rumors. It was something we had kind of expected, but then hadn't expected. Not like this. Not this sudden. But this is how things happened in the Army.

Tom explained he would be gone only ten days, maybe, but later on (he couldn't tell me how much later), he would be going back for a year, maybe longer.

"Déjà vu!" I blurted out incredulously. I didn't know what else to say. I just thought how eerie it was that twelve years ago in November, I sat on a similar couch in a similar house in Germany while my husband delivered to me a very similar message—he was deploying to Desert Storm.

However, my reactions to the years-apart messages were very different. The first time he broke the news, I broke down in tears. Tom had just been promoted to first lieutenant, and I was four months pregnant with our first daughter, Kristin. I felt helpless. I was going to miss him. I had no idea what I was going to do or how I was going to get through the pregnancy without him.

This time, I didn't cry, but I couldn't believe it was happening again. The kids were used to Daddy's being gone here and there for a few weeks or a couple of months, but for a whole year or more? That was a long time.

Suddenly, the motto I had adopted early on as a military wife came to mind: "You do what you've got to do." I could do this. We could do this.

I spent the next three days helping Tom get all the supplies, uniforms, and patches he would need for desert duty.

He came back from Kuwait after a week or so, but we knew he would be leaving again soon. We tried our best to get through two birthdays, Thanksgiving, and Christmas with his departure heavy on our minds.

It was a somber Friday morning in January. The girls and I were huddled in the front hallway with Tom and his gear. These would be our last few minutes with him until his return, date unknown.

"I still don't know why you don't want us to go down to battalion to say goodbye," I told him. But I did understand. I knew he didn't want to drag this whole thing out, trying to hold on to the last few minutes together, prolonging the moment when we would have to part.

"It's for the better. The kids don't need to miss school for this."

He smiled and hugged each of our daughters. "Be good. Take care of your mom for me."

Nicole, our youngest, began to cry.

Tom wore sand-colored boots and an unfamiliar, sand-colored uniform made from fabric that looked like chocolate chip cookie dough, according to our middle daughter, Sarah. I whisked a tear away with my hand, hoping I wouldn't totally lose it in front of my girls.

Tom turned to me with open arms. His face was red, and he was trying hard not to cry, but I could see my pain reflected in his face.

"I guess this is it," he said as he gave me a powerful embrace.

Our goodbye was passionately brief. He left through the front door. I fed the kids breakfast and took them to school.

My actions became mechanical after I dropped the girls off at school. I drove home, parked the car, and unlocked the door to the house. I went upstairs, took off my clothes. I turned on the faucet and stepped into the shower. The blast of warm water cascaded over my shoulders. I felt the release, and I wept. I bawled my head off. Once I got started, I couldn't stop. Just because I had done this before didn't mean it would be easier this time. I knew how to survive without him, but that didn't mean I was going to like it.

It took a couple of weeks for us to adjust to his being gone, to get into our own routine. It was evident that he was missing from our lives. The empty place at the dinner table, the way our dog aggressively barked at a knock on our door. Dad wasn't there to read at night, to tuck in his girls. The cat took to sleeping with me in our big empty bed.

The next few months I took lots of pictures of the girls and printed them to postcard-sized paper. The girls would write to their dad about the pictures they'd painted or tell him it had snowed. We baked peanut butter cookies, his favorite, and sent dozens of packages of goodies his way. But the thing that kept me going was our e-mails to each other. I looked forward to that daily note from him. And as long as I knew he was all right, I was all right.

I kept a journal, which helped me keep my head. I walked the dog, rode my bike, cross-country skied, rollerbladed, did yoga, lifted weights . . . whatever I could to keep the daily stresses to a minimum. (How do single moms do this all the time?) I decided I would focus on the day he would come home, even though I didn't know when that would be. It was comforting for me to know he would be home eventually. We would be a family again.

We were at the end of our tour in Germany and expecting orders to move back to the States that summer. In March, Tom sent me an e-mail that said to expect orders soon for Kansas. I was excited, but I worried that the Army would not allow anyone who was already deployed to leave theater even if they did have orders.

The orders came about the same time Tom was sent to Baghdad to cache weapons. He was nowhere near a computer or telephone. No more daily e-mails. A week later, I received a short, encrypted message e-mailed to me from the back of a truck somewhere in the desert saying he was okay. At the bottom of the message it said, "Do not reply to this message."

Great. I couldn't ask him what to do. We had orders to move, but I didn't know if he was coming home. Should I set up the appointment with transportation? What would happen if they packed up our stuff and put it on a ship, but Tom didn't come back? It was very possible that could happen, but I had to take the chance it wouldn't.

There is a saying in the Army: "War is hell, but moving is a close second." I had gone through three moves in the last four years in Germany. This time when the movers showed up, my work was already done. I was prepared for this move. And it seemed to be going fairly well.

It was a mild June day. The girls were upstairs playing computer games on the floor in the office. I sat outside in the grassy yard on my kitchen chair, reading a book. Inside the house, German-speaking packers rolled up my glassware in layers of thick paper and packed them into dish packs. From dispensers they wrenched packing tape and laid it across the cardboard box tops; the noise of the tape screeching through the open windows of the house picked at my nerves just a little. It was a sound I associated with every move. All day the tape screeched, and the boxes got packed up.

By the end of the day, we were all tired. The movers were to return in the morning to finish up. The girls were excited to sleep on blow-up mattresses on the floor that night. The house was empty except for some borrowed Army furniture. Everything that was important to us—our luggage, our important papers, anything I didn't want the movers to pack, including the telephone—was in the second-floor bathroom. It was a trick I had learned after hearing horror stories of movers packing up people's car keys or passports or even their garbage. If you locked it in the bathroom, it was safe.

I fell asleep that night, content in knowing the hardest part was almost over.

The cat was puking. The sounds of gagging pulled me out of my sleep. I was reluctant to get up for that. My brain was still asleep, but somewhere deep inside me I knew something was wrong. It usually didn't take that long for the cat to throw up.

The next thing I knew, I was standing over my youngest daughter, Nicole, who was lying on her air mattress in the hallway. Her back was arched, her eyes rolled up into the back of her head, her mouth was open. She was making guttural sounds as she convulsed.

"Are you okay? Nicole?" I heard myself say.

Nicole's body thrashed. She didn't answer.

"Nicole!"

Crap! I was not prepared for this!

Kristin and Sarah had come into the hallway. I barked at them both to find the phone book as I charged into the cluttered bathroom in search of the phone. By the time I got a nurse at the clinic on the line, Nicole's seizure had stopped. She had never had one before, so it was off to the German hospital in Weiden to get her checked out.

Nicole was a little tired, but she seemed fine. I made a quick call to the rear detachment to see if he could take care of the movers, and then I got Kristin and Sarah settled into the neighbors' house next door.

Next I drove twenty miles to the nearest hospital, where Nicole was diagnosed with benign focal epilepsy (a condition she would eventually outgrow) and sentenced to eight days in the hospital to monitor her medication. She shared a room with six other patients and their parents. I had a little mother's bed next to hers so I could stay with her overnight. Cartoon characters babbled in German on the overhead television all day. This was the absolute worst time for something like this to happen, but I was handling it. It would be okay.

Two days later, Tom quietly walked into Nicole's hospital room, a big smile on his face. He was tan and slim, wearing civilian clothes.

"Daddy!" she cried.

I couldn't believe my eyes; he was there in the room with us. We hugged. There was no fanfare, no balloons, no big noisy reception at the airport. It was enough that he was back safely with us.

Nicole had to stay in the hospital for six more days after that. Tom went home to take care of the other girls and to pack up the rest of the household goods while I stayed with Nicole. It was a long six days. But I did what I had to do, happily.

—*Amy Bladow Rivard*

On Time or Else

The twenty first-graders sat in a circle, some of them twitching, some of them whispering, almost all of them bored. Sonny, the class clown, reached over and pulled dress sashes, smiling broadly at the girls' dismay when their dresses came untied. Ignoring the antics, Mrs. West patiently explained, again, how the hour hand and the minute hand work on a clock.

She put the hour hand on the one and the minute hand on the twelve. Then she called on me. "Gladdy, what time does the clock say?"

The answer was so obvious it had to be a joke. Even Sonny could answer that one.

"It's thirteen hundred hours, ma'am."

My classmates looked at me and giggled into their cupped hands. Bobby and Jeff, mortal enemies, vying for the top spot in our Bumblebees reading group, laughed aloud and pointed at me, shaking their heads at my ignorance.

"No, Gladdy, not military time," said Mrs. West. "Regular time for regular people."

"Oh, okay. One o'clock, ma'am," I answered, my cheeks flaming red with embarrassment. I looked at the door. Could I run out and keep on going to the safety of home? I decided to stand my ground, another rule my father had taught me. "How do you know when it's military time and when it's regular time?"

Mrs. West didn't have an answer for that, and after nearly fifty years, neither do I. Brought up a military kid, I had the military way of thinking to rule my life, usually for the better, though even today I endure mockery for my obsession with clocks, calendars, and lists.

Right after I was born, our family was posted to Frankfurt, Germany, by the U.S. Army. My father was in charge of the escort of the trains that ran in and out of the western sector of then-isolated Berlin after World War II. He prided himself on the precision of those trains, and always, he has been a man who has run things by the clock.

As my brother Davey and I grew up, we knew there was time in every day for every task to be accomplished. Vacuum and wash the dishes before school. Feed the dog, feed the pigeons, and set the table before homework in the afternoon. We stood at the doors of our rooms for inspection on Saturdays at 7:00 A.M. sharp, holding our breath, hoping to pass. Reaching for a compliment would have been too much to ask. A simple nod of the head would clear us. And yes, that quarter had better bounce off the mitered corners of the blanket, or it was KP and latrine duty for the weekend.

This regimen wasn't in effect only when we were little kids. On prom night, Davey dragged himself home at about 3:00 A.M. I heard him come in, envying the thrills of dancing in the dark at a big hotel, wearing formal attire, his girlfriend's ruffled, hoopskirted prom dress, and their after-prom dinner at San Diego's famous Bali Hai, with its legendary views and ambrosial nonalcoholic fruit drinks.

My father, too, surely heard my brother's late arrival, for at 6:00 A.M., Poppa got on the intercom and began whistling, "Reveille," followed by the stentorian tones only my father could achieve: "Rise and shine! Rise and shine! Swimming practice begins at 0700 hours. You will be there, my son."

From my brother's room I heard what might have been a swear word. He got up. He made practice.

The most trouble I ever got myself into occurred because I let my heart rule my head. As a high school sophomore, in love for the first time, I consciously chose to stay after school to watch my boyfriend compete in a cross-country meet, knowing I would be in trouble for coming home late. But for that moment, I didn't care. I wanted to stay, to be there, for Steve. We didn't have cell phones, and I couldn't reach my working parents, as they would already be on the freeway, heading home.

Steve crossed the finish line nearly last. He bent over and vomited. Frankly, I was sorry I was there to witness his humiliation. The tables turned to my humiliation when I tromped home, two hours late, to find my father standing at the door, tapping his watch and wiggling his foot.

"Gladdy, to your room! What were you thinking?"

No excuse I could have offered would have worked. I told the truth. I ended up confined to quarters, missing the first football game of the season, my first date at night with Steve.

In our house, being on time was the golden ticket to privileges. It's funny that as an adult, my brother, a CEO who had been punctual as he made his way to the top, now makes a statement by being late to everything, from office meetings to weddings. Until my mom died, we held a lottery at Christmas for what time he would finally show up.

Me? I'm always a half hour to an hour early, even if it's just lunch across town. If an engagement takes me from Los Angeles to San Diego, a long drive through some of the worst traffic in the country, I factor in enough time for traffic, weather, and car breakdowns. I am never late, not to a casual lunch and not on a long-distance trek. If I am ever late, people will know that I've been in a serious accident, that my flight was delayed, or that I'm dead.

I also know that my military training made me the reliable teacher that I was. In thirty-two years of teaching high school, I never arrived tardy to a class or to a school day. We finished the curriculum and had time for extras. My classes received their essays back on the date I said they would, whether that meant I stayed up until midnight, worked all weekend, or graded papers on New Year's Day during the Rose Bowl game. I was a yearbook adviser for twenty-five of those years. It should be no surprise that my staff never missed one deadline and that we never had to come in to work after school or on weekends, as the yearbook staffs of the other high schools did. We used the class period for work, though we laughed our way through the tension. And in all my classes, there was joy in accomplishing so much, though I admit there was grumbling too, sometimes from parents.

I make lists. If I don't do everything on my list, I get agitated and move the item to number one on the next day's list. My husband is a laissez-faire, never-plan-anything type of guy, providing a nice healthy balance to my small obsessions. We're good for one another. We certainly laugh at one another's foibles. I avoid making "honey do" lists for the man, and he says, "Okay, Dad," to remind me to ease up when I'm grabbing my car keys before he's had time to even head for the shower. I still make lists for myself. And by golly, I get a lot done.

Take heart, those whose homes run under the martial law of the military stopwatch. There's much to be gained by organizing time to accomplish set goals.

As a child and as a teen, I would never have admitted this, but I say it now without the slightest hesitation. Thank you, Daddy, for helping me to become the responsible and productive woman I am today.

—*Eileen Clemens Granfors*

Not Navy Knots

"I'm home! I got it!" my husband called as he burst in through the front door of the Quonset hut, waving a large envelope.

Our daughter, Dee, raced toward him, blonde curls bouncing, arms raised. Howard leaned over, scooped up the four-year-old, and swung her around. We all hugged as we danced around the room—a circle of joy.

"Are you packed?" Howard asked.

"Almost," I said.

"I am, except my scooter," Dee chirped. "What'd you get, Daddy?"

Howard plopped down on the nearby sofa, sat Dee on his lap, and patted the spot beside him. "Come here, hon," he said. "Open it. You read it aloud."

Forget packing! Seizing the big manila envelope, I ripped it open, took a deep breath, and read:

HONORABLE DISCHARGE from the UNITED
STATES NAVY

This is to certify that Howard Norvel Simms, a
Shipfitter Second Class USSNR, is Honorably Discharged from the U S. Naval Personnel Separation
Center U.S.N.B., T.L., San Pedro, California, and
from the Naval Service of the United States this
14th day of April, 1946.

J. F. Heiney

I glanced up at my husband and daughter. Their
faces glowed with happiness. "I'll put this in the bottom of the suitcase and read it later," I said as I rose
quickly. "We've got packing to do."

All the furniture and furnishings in the Quonset
hut, from the couch to the dishes in the cupboards and
the linens on the beds, belonged to the Navy. The only
things we'd be taking with us were our personal possessions, and those were few. This had been our home
away from home for the past three months. Happy
months. A vacation for me. In a way, I hated to leave
California—the ocean, the sunshine, the misty rain.

Howard placed Dee on the floor and gave her a
quick kiss on the forehead. "I'm headed for the base
to see if I can round up some used tires. Ours are

bald. Finish packing, and we'll load the car tonight and be off early in the morning."

As I watched my husband stride out the door, looking back to flash a grin my way, I thought he looked especially handsome. His smile displayed his one dimple. His blue eyes sparkled beneath his high forehead. A white sailor's hat, cocked jauntily to one side, let wisps of wheat-colored hair escape.

Dee tugged at my arm. "Does Grandma know we're coming home?"

I stopped packing; I hadn't had time to even think of that. "If I can find paper, pencil, and envelopes, we'll write a note to both of your grandmas. Then we'll walk to the post office. I could use a bit of fresh air and exercise; we'll be riding all day tomorrow."

"Can you still write 'free' instead of using a stamp, Mama?"

"Yes, one more time. As long as I write Port Hueneme, California, as the return address and your daddy's serial number on the envelope."

I smoothed my daughter's sandy-colored bangs in a gesture of love. Almost nonexistent eyebrows didn't detract from her sky-blue eyes. The child's thin smile seemed ready to burst into a childish giggle. She had been exposed to so many changes in her short life. *Will she always feel this secure?* I wondered.

"Did I ever tell you about the letter that was lost?" I began. "I'd written your daddy when he was in New Jersey. The letter traveled all over Europe and then came back almost six months later."

"Yes, Mama, I remember. Daddy was in a line to go overseas, and they stopped calling out names just when they came to his, but they sent his mail anyway."

"You have a good memory for a little girl." Dee beamed at the praise as she hopped around the room in her excitement.

"Go to your room now and look in the closet and drawers to see if we've left anything behind." I had the paper and pen in my hand but could use a little quiet.

Dee hesitated in the doorway before turning back and asking, "Can I make the hugs and kisses?"

"Oh yes, you must send Xs and Os. Your grand-mas miss you."

My thoughts slid back to December 7, when we had heard the news that the Japanese had bombed Pearl Harbor. I was twenty years old and nine months preg-nant with Dee. Who would have dreamed she would be four before the fighting ended and the men returned?

Later that evening, when I carried the first load to the car, my hand flew to my mouth and my eyes opened wide. "Where did all this stuff come from?" I exclaimed.

The floorboard was full of metal boxes and all sorts of paraphernalia. My heart sank. I looked helplessly at my husband.

"We'll give away that junk you bought at the Navy's white elephant sale," Howard suggested. "We won't need that small chest of drawers once we're home."

"It's mine!" Dee began crying. The child loved the cheap furniture, cardboard wallpapered with pretty animals.

"I'm using it to hold clothes for the trip home. Stick it somewhere," I said. "Where'd you say those tool boxes came from?"

My husband's face brightened. "The Navy sells surplus tools, fifteen dollars for a hundred bucks worth of tools. I bought two boxes—and this duffel bag of fatigues. They were going to burn these perfectly good clothes; I'll need them for work," he explained.

Sweat dripped from his face. "The tarpaulin and army cots are like new. We can use them to camp on the way home. I bought cans of food at the commissary, too."

He looked as pleased as I felt alarmed. He flipped the curlers I'd forgotten to remove from my hair. "How you can sleep in those things?" he asked.

Then he clasped my hand and squeezed it. "Come around back and see what else: three used spare tires, and they've more tread on them than ours. It's a long way to drive on threadbare tires." He led me to the rear of the Plymouth and proudly patted the tires. "The fellas tied these behind our spare and left enough rope for me to add Dee's scooter."

Our 1934 Plymouth didn't have a trunk, so the spare was bolted to the back. A jack, tire tools, and a foot pump were pushed under the back seat.

"Are you going to leave those two bicycles on top?" I shook my head in dismay. "The roof of the car might cave in."

"Naw. These old cars are made of heavy metal. Bicycles don't weigh much. We'll be glad to have them in Festus," he reassured me. "Come on! Let's finish packing the car before it gets dark."

How the man managed to crowd everything in I'll never know. Every crook and cranny was filled, and the back seat was now level with the windows. Over it all we spread blankets and pillows. Early the next morning, Dee crawled in this space with her doll. I climbed in on the driver's side and slid under the steering wheel to the middle of the seat; the passenger door was blocked with rolls of canvas, duffle bags, and army cots. My feet shared the floorboard with cans of food. No matter. We were happy. We were on our way home to Missouri, 1,500 miles away!

I can't remember if gas was still being rationed or if the Navy had given us ration stamps for the journey. What I do remember of that early April in 1946 is that we met very few cars on the road and that gas was scarce and new tires were unavailable.

As we drove that first day, Howard said, "The mechanics at the base warned that our car has a flat crankshaft. It may not make the trip if we don't baby it."

"Oh," I said. "How do you baby a car?"

"Drive forty miles per hour. I'll set the throttle so we cruise at that speed. Sit back and enjoy the scenery."

He took his foot off the gas pedal and leaned over, slipped his arm around my shoulder, and pulled me close. "Gee, it feels good to be leaving the base. On the trip to California, I worried we'd be late and I'd get locked in the brig. The Navy tolerates no foul-ups. Now, I'm free!"

"But you're still in uniform," Dee puzzled.

"Yes, sweetie. I kept my blues to honor those still serving. After today, I'll wear them only for parades."

Two hours later, a car passed us. A young woman on the passenger side waved her arm and pointed toward our back seat. We waved back. As the black Chevrolet zoomed past us, she stuck her head out the window and flung her arm toward us several more times.

"Friendly lady, isn't she, Mama?"

"A good-looking man in uniform always impresses women. I don't think she meant to flirt. After all, I am in the car." I glanced over at my husband but said no more. I moved a tad closer to him. He gave my shoulder a quick squeeze.

"Let's sing," I suggested.

We sang every song we could think of with the word "home" in the lyrics. A good hour later, still creeping along at forty miles per hour, we were almost hypnotized into a stupor by the sameness of the road.

Dee was so quiet I thought she was asleep until she spoke. "Here comes a red car."

A convertible with the top down overtook us and pulled alongside. Inside were four young ladies wearing halter tops beneath smiling faces, hair blowing in the wind. The driver honked the horn, slowed her car to match its speed to ours and held it there a full sixty seconds; all the while, its occupants were gesturing wildly and calling something only the wind heard. One last honk and they sped away.

"Really!" I muttered indignantly.

Howard enjoyed my jealousy immensely; his blue eyes twinkled as a mischievous grin burst into full-blown laughter.

A few minutes later, he glanced my way and winked. "My rear-view mirror tells me another vehicle is behind us. People are friendly around here. We must be coming to a town. I'd better buy gas at the next stop."

An older couple appeared to be straining to pass, honking incessantly. They, too, waved at us enthusiastically and pointed.

"Do you think I'm getting a flat?" Howard pondered. "The car isn't pulling to the right or left, though."

He stopped at the first service station. We all crawled out to stretch our legs.

"Come see," he called from the back.

Behind the car, three used tires and one scooter rested on the gravel driveway. By the looks of them, they'd been dragged behind on the paved road for a good long while. Though still secured by the ropes, miles and miles of scooting had worn the rubber on the tires down to the bare sides. They were useless!

My husband almost doubled over with laughter, slapping his legs. I didn't share his humor.

"I must say you are taking this well," I grumbled. "I thought the Navy taught all sailors to work with ropes and tie secure knots. These are definitely not Navy knots."

"Navy knots or not, I'm too happy to be upset. Just think—the war is finally over, I'm discharged, and I'm taking my girls home to Missouri. Hop in! Let's go home!"

"Can we make it without the tires, Daddy?" Dee asked.

He looked back at her worried little face with its apple-pink cheeks. "Sure, little one. There is no way I won't chauffeur my favorite girls safely home. Do you remember the CB's motto?"

Dee nodded.

"Okay, let's recite it together. Ready? Loud and clear, at the count of three: one . . . two . . . three.

"The difficult we do right away. The impossible takes a little longer."

—Verna L. Simms

A (Nearly) Perfect Christmas

"Hurry up, honey!" My husband held my coat. "We have to leave for the airport to pick up our Christmas guests now or no one will be here to enjoy your decorations. Let's go." He tried to be firm, but his excitement as a stepfather mirrored my own.

He was right: Our home stood ready for Christmas. Guest room—special tree decorated for four-year-old granddaughter, Madeline: check. Bathroom—fragrant body lotions, special soaps, and pretty towels for beloved daughter-in-law, Julie: check. Outside lights—a shimmering winter wonderland gleaming on our little Texas hill: check. Christmas tree—decorated floor to ceiling with a twenty-four-inch yellow bow nestled in the center for son, Frank, our Marine Gunny Sergeant stationed somewhere in the Iraqi desert: check. War or no war, our family would be together for Christmas this year.

On the way to the airport, I reflected on life with children in the military. I am an ordinary civilian mother, but the Marine Corps had controlled me for the past fifteen years. My son enlisted—as one of the few good men—straight out of high school. Then my young, unmarried Marine deployed to the Persian Gulf War in 1990. Dismal is the way I remember that Christmas.

A few years later, my son took Julie for his wife. Delighted, and determined to outsmart the military, I embarked on a new adventure of airline travel, flying to wherever they were stationed, whenever I could. Then, on a lovely summer day in 2000, my son and daughter-in-law brought forth beautiful Madeline Elizabeth—at which point I should have purchased stock in several airlines. In spite of the Marine Corps, my world circled around my granddaughter. But despite all the trips we made to Marine Corps bases, and with the trips our military children made to Texas, we had not been together for Christmas since Frank graduated boot camp in 1989.

Early in the summer of 2004, my son and his family visited us in Texas. At the time, he knew his tank company would soon deploy to the war zone, but he did not want his mother to know. He'd forgotten I was an experienced military mom, and I smelled imminent deployment. However, we pretended all was well throughout their week's stay, and the word "war" never crossed our lips.

In midsummer, Frank's company received official orders for his first deployment since he and Julie had married. By then, Julie had become a seasoned Marine wife, and I had survived sending my son to war once before, so we thought we knew the ropes. We soon learned that every war and every deployment comes with its own unique terror and that even battle-ready Marines have to face down unexpected fears.

Julie inquired several times, "Have you told your mom?"

Frank tartly gave her his standard response: "I haven't had time."

The summer droned on, and Frank spent most of his time away from home, training, practicing, teaching, and preparing. He and the men entrusted to his care knew they would be ready when departure came, but he went to work before Madeline was up and returned after she was in bed.

Julie did the mommy and the daddy things as well as the good-Marine-wife things, like attending meetings to learn how to handle the horrible "what-ifs." She kept Madeline busy with summer activities and pasted on the "everything is okay" smile. With her daddy gone so much, four-year-old

Madeline grew restless, had nightmares, became sassy, and cried easily.

One evening Frank got home early, bone-tired but eager to see his family. He called out his ritual greeting, "Hi, Squeaky! Daddy's home."

No response.

Madeline did not run to meet him. She did not stop her play or look up. Instead, with her head down, she said, "Go on back to the Marines, Gunny. You don't live here anymore; you live with them."

Then she ran to her bedroom and slammed the door shut behind her. Separation had arrived in all its meanness.

My son walked slowly down the hall and said through the closed door, "I love you, Madeline." The tired Marine sat down on the floor, leaned against the door, and said, "I'll wait here for you."

Before she could come out for a tearful hug and to be rocked to sleep by her daddy, she played with her horses for a long while, pretending she lived alone with only her horses, far, far away. Life had changed, and Madeline did not know why.

Finally, in August, Julie said, "Okay. Pick up the phone. Your mom survived your first deployment; she isn't dumb. She needs to hear it from you."

I hopped a plane the next week, and the four of us had an extraordinary week together. Even though we did not talk of war things in front of Madeline, children, too, smell war.

Every morning Madeline would say, "Don't worry, Memaw. I'm a big girl, and I'll take care of Mommy when Daddy goes to war."

Every night she came to me for a hug, and I said, "Sweet dreams, Madeline. I love you."

She would giggle, squeeze me tight, and say, "Sweet dreams, Memaw. I love you, too."

Madeline started preschool about the time Frank shipped out, and Julie's confidence grew that they'd all make it through deployment okay. A week later, Madeline brought her up short while Julie was tucking her into bed one night.

After their three-story bedtime ritual, Julie said, "It's time to say our prayers."

Madeline flipped over, pulled the blanket over her head, and said, "I'm not talking to God. I asked him every night for four days to send my daddy home, and he hasn't done it!"

Once Madeline was finally asleep, Julie went to her own empty bed. She prayed. She cried. Both she and Madeline needed reassurance, needed to be bound up by loving cords that reached beyond war, separation, emptiness, and fear. They needed family. And so she decided that she and Madeline would come to Texas to spend Christmas with us.

Much to Madeline's delight and mine, the planning was on. Julie and I kept telephone lines busy and e-mails flying as our plans unfolded. Her friends had another opinion. "Are you actually going to visit your in-laws without your husband? Julie, you've lost your mind!" Confident of her status with us—my son called her "Mom's Spoiled One"—Julie laughed and kept planning.

The day before their flight, Madeline suddenly rebelled. "I'm not going to Texas." Fuming, she took things out of the suitcase as fast as Julie packed.

"Madeline! You love going to Memaw's house. Of course we are going."

Madeline sat on the floor sobbing. Gathering her brokenhearted child in her arms, Julie rocked and sang until Madeline's tears subsided. Between hiccups, Madeline sputtered, "But I've never been to Texas without my daddy. I don't know if we're 'posed to do that!"

Julie's courage dissolved into tears, too. But the next day they boarded the plane.

At the San Antonio International Airport, there were huge numbers of military personnel everywhere, but my husband and I ignored them. We didn't stop to say, "Thank you." We didn't wonder if they were arriving home or departing for battle. We just grabbed Julie and Madeline and hugged until we couldn't breathe. Some of my children were in my arms. Madeline slept most of the way from the city airport to our rural community, but she bounced wide awake when the twinkling lights on our hill came into view.

Our twelve days of Christmas spilled over with activities; time flew like the wind. Aunts, uncles, cousins, friends, and neighbors came to call; young playmates appeared; and family rituals abounded. Madeline and I explored every inch of Fredericksburg, an original Christmas Tinsel Town, and Julie shopped unhampered.

One night Julie took a long bath after she put Madeline to bed. Suddenly, Madeline ran down the hall calling, "Memaw, Memaw!" I scooped her up, and she said, "I couldn't find you. You forgot to tell me to have sweet dreams!"

I hugged her. "I'm so sorry. Madeline, I love you. Please have sweet dreams."

She giggled, squeezed me tight, and said, "I love you, too. Have sweet dreams, Memaw."

Then the dreaded but mandatory Christmas ear infection hit with a bang, and Madeline was miserable. One night I sent an exhausted Julie to bed, and Madeline and I snuggled in the rocking chair by the Christmas tree. Halfway through a story, I felt tears on her face.

"Does your ear hurt?" I asked.

"No," she whimpered, then buried her tear-streaked face in my shoulder. After a while she said, "I need my daddy. I don't know what to do without him."

With tears on my own face I began telling her "when-daddy-was-a-little-boy" stories. I showed Madeline each ornament on the tree that was special to her daddy: the stocking from his first teacher, the wooden teddy bear made by an aunt, the Santa bell his grandmother had given him. I carried her around the house, talking about the pictures of her, her daddy, and all our family.

Back in the rocking chair, Madeline yawned. "It's okay, Memaw. I'm a big girl now." She slept peacefully.

Normal life quickly returned. My teenage grandson brought school friends to visit, and the girls sat on the floor for hours playing My Little Pony with Madeline. Our family prayed together every day. We read books, told stories, and cooked.

Then, for fifteen wonderful minutes on Christmas Eve afternoon, Christmas stopped in mid-sentence when our Marine telephoned Texas from the war zone in Iraq.

Julie hung up the phone. My son's dad and stepmother arrived with hugs and Christmas cookies.

Julie and my daughter went to Christmas Eve mass. Even Santa found his way to Madeline's Memaw's house in Texas.

Then, too soon, Christmas was over.

"We have to leave for the airport, honey." My husband's smile was as phony as my own.

Madeline had regained her usual self-assurance, so at the airport I said, "I want you to hold my hand when we get out of the car."

"Okay, Memaw. I'm a big girl, you know, but I'll do that for you."

Clinging to each other, we dragged our steps, trying to delay saying goodbye. True to our rituals of many years standing, Julie, Madeline, and I hugged and hugged, and cried and hugged again, until we reached security and I couldn't go any farther.

"Be a big girl, Madeline."

"I will. You be a big girl, too, Memaw." She touched my face, then fled to her mother's arms.

I wiped away tears as I watched them go and smiled in spite of myself. The war had not cheated us out of our Christmas, and this time, as we left the airport, my husband and I looked directly at every military person who passed by. We smiled and said, "God bless. Thank you."

—Liz Hoyt Eberle

Stressed and Blessed

Married twenty-five years to an "I'll never leave California" high school music teacher turned military aviator, I live in a continual state of surprise.

"Ride with me to take Matthew to school this morning," my husband, Ben, said to me over the breakfast table.

"Okay," I answered.

"Good morning, girl," my father said as he walked into the kitchen.

"Morning, Dad. I'll be right back," I said as I hugged him.

I knew how much he missed me. When Ben and I married, my dad asked him to promise he would never take me far from California. It has been the only promise Ben hasn't kept.

I changed from pajamas into jeans and a T-shirt, went outside, and got in the truck with my husband and son.

Ben was leaving on a temporary duty trip to Utah. His job required frequent stints away from home. Like other military couples, much travel, frequent moves, and time apart took a toll on our marriage. Under the continual stress of military separations, we fought often. In a year punctuated with his absences, I had struggled even more lately with feeling neglected. Intellectually, I knew my husband loved me, but emotionally I felt unloved.

The visiting relatives in our home meant that riding with Ben to drop Matthew off was my opportunity for a few minutes to talk with Ben before his morning flight.

"Love you, Mom," Matthew said as we dropped him off at school.

Matthew didn't say goodbye to his dad, but I didn't notice. On the ride back home, my husband passed by the turn for our street.

"I need to get home," I said. "I want to make breakfast for Dad."

Ben didn't look at me.

Minutes later I said, "You passed the street. I need to get home." I felt my teeth clench in anger at more time spent away from my dad and sister.

"Where are we going?" I pressed. My irritation with him for not going straight back home just exacerbated the resentment I felt for him leaving me again.

"You'll just have to wait and see."

Did he have to be so smug about it?

As he drove further past our neighborhood, my mind raced from the thought of my waiting family to my to-do list for an upcoming church conference. My body filled with tension.

"Where are you taking me? I have to get home now."

Keenly aware of my mood and impatience, he paused thoughtfully and then said, "We're going to Norfolk."

The airport was in Norfolk, an hour's drive away. He usually left his car in long-term parking for his return trip on military travel.

"I don't have time to drop you off at the airport. You need to take me home," I insisted.

"You're going with me."

My stomach muscles tightened. How could he? "No, I told you I couldn't go on this trip."

Earlier in the month, he had asked if I wanted to join him on this trip, and I declined. My face flushed. I felt manipulated.

"I came with you to drop off Matthew and to be with you for a few minutes before you left. I can't go with you to Utah. I don't want to go. I don't even have anything with me."

"You don't need anything. I packed for you."

As I looked down at my wrinkled T-shirt and jeans, I boiled with emotion. My ears felt hot. The muscles in my back tensed.

"I didn't shower. These clothes are dirty. I just slipped them on to ride with you to take Matthew to school. I haven't even had my estrogen this morning."

He knew what that could mean. A battle with ovarian cancer had left me in daily need of hormone replacement therapy.

"It's in your suitcase in the trunk."

"Well, you'd better pull over now and get it."

Wise man that he is, he did. We stopped at a gas station, bought a bottle of water, and I downed the water and anti-wench pill.

Few words punctuated the silence during the next hour as we rode to the airport. Seething with resentment, I glared at Ben. He looked straight ahead as he drove.

Ben parked the car and unloaded the luggage he had thoughtfully packed for his unsuspecting wife. Speechless, I stared at him as we walked from the parking garage to the check-in terminal.

At the counter, dressed in my frumpy travel costume, the counter agent took one look at me and beamed her 8:00 A.M. smile. "Good morning, where are we going today?"

I spun around to face Ben. "Ask him."

Taking the tickets from him, she punched in our flight information. "Mrs. Hines, let's see, you are going to Honolulu."

"Hawaii?"

A grin spread across my husband's face. Anger and resentment dissolved into surprise, as I remembered our upcoming twenty-fifth wedding anniversary. Of course he knew I wouldn't want to travel to the desert. Emotions and thoughts swirled inside me as I realized my family and friends were in on the grand surprise.

"Happy anniversary, hon. Do you still love me?"

I squeezed him, as the ticket agent looked on, smiling.

As we walked to the gate, I reached for Ben's hand. Fifteen hours later, we arrived to begin our silver anniversary adventure on Oahu.

The Hawaiian breeze carried the scent of plumeria blooms to greet us. We breathed in fresh-scented sea air. This was not the desert in Utah. I felt God's love touch my heart and my marriage in an intimate way.

Ben and I spent the next seven days enjoying each other and our island adventure. The week included a sunrise hike at Diamond Head Volcano, snorkeling in Hanauma Bay, and a real luau.

The previous week, I had had it with military life. I felt neglected and resentful of my husband. I struggled to navigate through my feelings. It's hard to resent a man who lives each day willing to die for his country and our freedoms. Ben needed a break from the demands of duty, and so did our marriage. His deployment to the Pacific created an opportunity for a special time together for us. It reminded a duty-weary spouse that feelings are not always truth and that, for all its stresses and sacrifices, military life includes benefits and blessings, too.

—*Donna Lee Hines*

Long Distance with My Brother

I stopped by my brother's house on his day off. From his front door, he waved me inside.

"Robert's going to call in a few minutes," he said. "You're just in time."

What a treat! Our younger brother, Robert, a sergeant in the Army Reserves, was in Kuwait. His veterinary unit had been deployed as part of Iraqi Freedom to care for military dogs and to inspect food and water supplies for the troops. He e-mailed often, but I had not talked with him since he'd left Independence, Missouri, several months before. Precious phone time was reserved for his wife and kids, and, as I discovered that day, for my other brother, Bo. Bo is a year younger than I am and six years older than Robert. They both are letter carriers and share an interest in military history.

I hurried inside, and we waited at the kitchen table for the phone to ring, both of us eager to hear how our forty-three-year-old brother was faring in the war on terror. Robert is the blond baby brother we adored and spoiled; the kid who graduated from Tonka trucks to plastic soldiers and tanks; the boy who built model ships for the sole purpose of destroying them, reenacting naval battles in the creek behind our house. We missed him.

Five years earlier, Robert had been deployed to Kosovo, a climate colder and less hostile than the Iraqi war zone. During that deployment, at Robert's suggestion, we enlisted friends and coworkers to collect winter hats, scarves, and mittens to send to the children he came in contact with during the course of his duties there. He accompanied the chaplain when they delivered the brightly colored woolens, and he forwarded photos and a thank-you letter from the commander to us.

During this current deployment, I gave myself the assignment of documenting Robert's teenagers' activities. I videotaped his son's high school graduation, made a DVD, and shipped it off to prove that, yes, Robbie did receive a diploma. Then I spent the next two months videotaping his daughter's softball games and compiling the videos to send off to the absentee coach. When I was videotaping these events, the people being taped often would grimace . . . until I said, "This is for Robert." Then, suddenly, everyone wanted to say hi to him and didn't mind being recorded after all.

Robert's e-mails to us gave the impression that this mission was a lark, more like a summer camp adventure than a military deployment. But we knew better. The light-hearted nature of his correspondence was typical Robert. In fact, even when he is home, it is sometimes hard to know how he feels about things.

Maybe it is because I'm the oldest of five siblings and Robert the youngest, coupled with the seven-year age difference between us, that makes it difficult for us to communicate seriously. Robert was still in grade school when I left home for college. By the time he joined the Army, I was living 250 miles away and had missed watching him grow up. Maybe he thinks I might still be mad about his playing his electric guitar too loudly when my one-year-old was trying to take a nap during our visit home one Christmas. Or maybe he thinks I hold a grudge for that long-distance phone bill he ran up calling his girlfriend the summer he came to St. Louis to stay with us for a week. Perhaps it's just how it is between us, but it doesn't change the fact that I am proud of him and worry about him while he is gone.

So today, though I was excited, I was also surprisingly nervous that I might have an unexpected chance to talk with my youngest brother. What would I say? We were painting his house while he was gone; I could talk about that. I wondered what exactly his unit was doing over there; I could ask about that. I worried about his safety; I could tell him to be careful.

When the phone finally rang, Bo talked with him first while I eavesdropped on their conversation. What do my two brothers talk about long, long distance in the middle of a war? Post office gossip, I discovered.

Finally Bo said, "Linda's here. You want to talk to her?"

I was ready to grab the phone. I would not have been surprised if Robert said no. After all, of the five of us kids, he is the most like our grandfather, who was an insufferable tease. But the time delay on the line, annoying during the rest of the conversation, gave me the chance to start talking.

Robert didn't share any Army secrets with me during the call. He said he would be e-mailing more photographs soon and he appreciated the newspaper clippings about the Kansas City Chiefs that I had been sending him. We didn't talk long, but I was reassured to hear the teasing tone of his voice still intact.

Before we said goodbye, he mentioned that it was a lovely evening there in the desert. Later that night, sitting on my deck, I watched the moon rise. It, of course, was the same full moon my brother had admired while we talked. That beautiful moon and our unexpected visit on the phone seemed to bridge the distance between us.

Now, three years later, another yellow ribbon is tied around the maple tree in the front yard. Robert is in Afghanistan. This time, his e-mails are a bit more serious, but he lets me know when a full moon is coming my way. I watch for it. It brings my brother just a little closer to me, to home.

—*Linda Gammon*

Looking for Home

Even though I've lived in North Carolina longer than I've lived anywhere else, when someone asks me where I'm from, I always answer, "I grew up in a military family." The person usually nods and says, "Oh, an Army brat," as if that's all they need to know.

Maybe I offer up that detail because I want to reveal the fragmented nature of my childhood or the fact that I have no permanent home. Maybe it's because I grew up with no clear sense of myself. Being the youngest of four children, I was a chameleon, always looking for someone to show me how to be, how to act. I studied my sister and two brothers for clues. Because my early life was segmented by moves, when the family packed up and the scenery changed, my life changed, too.

My parents eventually settled on the coast of North Carolina and lived there for more than twenty years. Regardless, I never called Morehead City home, probably because I was still reeling from the loss of my other two homes, Panama and Florida, and the selves I'd left behind in each of those places.

It didn't help that we came to North Carolina when I was fifteen and in the tenth grade. My own body was changing, developing curves, becoming a stranger. And I could hardly understand the deep coastal accents of most of the people in Morehead City. "Would you mind repeating that?" I'd say when talking to a classmate on the phone. "One more time. A little slower, please." I had to concentrate to understand basic phrases and colloquialisms like, "We're gonna carry Mama to the store," or "Pete's feeling ill about that." I'd picture Mama being hoisted on someone's shoulders or Pete lying in bed with the flu before the true meanings dawned on me. When I was slow to respond in a voice with no detectable accent, I was confronted with funny looks and questions, "Where are you from, anyway? One of those northern states?" When I shook my head and answered, "No, I just moved from the Panama Canal Zone," most kids backed away. I was too shy to follow up.

The Canal Zone had been filled with other kids from military families, all nationalities, kids who had lived all over the world. The Zone was an artificial community, a ten-mile boundary on either side of the canal. The military housing could have been anywhere, except that the homes were surrounded by palm trees, jungle, and tropical birds. The people who lived there shared a sense of displacement, a sense of not belonging to any one part of the world.

In Morehead City, most of the kids had parents, grandparents, and great-grandparents who lived within a few blocks or miles of each other. They shared Sunday dinners and holidays. They had a deep love of the coastal islands. Their ancestors had made livings off the sea as fishermen or as restaurant or dock workers. Many of the kids had never been out of North Carolina, nor did they have a desire to leave.

By the time we moved there, three of my four grandparents had passed away—my father's parents, who lived in Tampa, and my mother's father, who had worked in New York City. We were lucky to see my maternal grandmother once a year during the summer at her home in White Plains, New York. Even my immediate family had shrunk. One brother was off at college in another state, and my sister was living in Florida. My mother took a part-time job with the local newspaper, and my other brother started working part-time at the hospital. When I came home from school, the house seemed hollow. Even though I was back on U.S. soil, I couldn't have felt more foreign.

Jacksonville, Florida, was my Eden. I lived there from the age of two until I was nine, riding my bike up and down Avondale Avenue under oak trees draped in Spanish moss. Summers stretched endlessly, and I knew the boundaries of my life—the park to the north, my friend Susie's house to the south, the creek where Bill and I collected tadpoles to the east, the house covered in ivy to the west. My siblings were always nearby. From under the azalea bushes where I collected roly-polies, I could see my sister twirling her baton and hear the tap-tap of her tennis shoes on the pavement as she practiced majorette routines. My brothers ran races across the front lawn. One perfected his putt-putt stroke while the other walked on stilts and I hopscotched down the sidewalk. There was always someone to call to, to say, "Hey! Watch this!" and someone to run to when I skinned my knee.

Even my parents played tennis in the street, batting balls back and forth over an imaginary net. Sometimes they set up a card table for the cotton candy machine under the shade of the oak tree. My mother poured colored sugar into the mouth of the contraption while we wound paper wands through wisps of blue and pink. We created fragile globes, passed them out to neighbors who walked by. I can still taste the sweetness of those days.

My father says I cried when he made the announcement at the dinner table that we were leaving Florida. I didn't want to give up the only world I knew. Daddy says he lured me down to Panama with the promise of a pony.

That's his story. I never saw that I had a choice. I was plunked down in a strange world where dark-skinned guards saluted my father as we passed through the gates of Fort Clayton and Howard Air Force Base. Within the confines of chain-link fence, I couldn't tell one home from another, one neighborhood from the next. All the houses were white with red tile roofs, most of them duplexes over open-air carports with stairs running up both sides. It would be easy to get lost in that place.

We arrived during the rainy season. Gardens were overgrown with bougainvillea and hibiscus blooms that seemed obscenely huge and bright. Shrubs with enormous waxy leaves looked like they might swallow a child if one got too close. What was there to do but climb in the car with my father when he said, "Let's go to the stables."

The pony, Charlie, turned out to be a Panamanian bush pony with no manners and even less training. My brothers and I took turns riding him at Fort Clayton Riding Club, until he dumped us all so many times we refused to do anything but stand beside his stall and feed him carrots. My father eventually took the hint and traded Charlie for Cochise, a sweet pony with a reputation for taking care of children. I spent long hours brushing his white coat, combing his long white tail, and tracing the shape of his ears with my fingers. The air from his nostrils felt warm in my hands. I rode bareback into the jungle, galloping past saw grass and cutter ants. Cochise's hooves made deep impressions in the red clay hills.

I never cried when we left Panama, even though I think that move was the most difficult for me. I left my pony behind, along with a part of me. I tried to be strong like my father, to look forward instead of back. I told myself it was exciting to be moving again, to discover a new place, to have new experiences. But at night I dreamed of Cochise. Over and over I returned to the Fort Clayton Riding Club, ran to my pony's stall, hugged him tight around the neck, and murmured into his mane that I would never leave him again. "I promise, I'll be back," I'd whisper. "I'm so sorry I left you." I'd wake with my eyes crusted shut from night tears.

Years later, when my husband, Joel, and I moved from Texas to Huntersville, North Carolina, just outside of the city of Charlotte, I told him I never wanted to move again. We built a house on eleven acres of land and moved my horse, Crimson, into a new barn on the property. I worked as a freelance writer and taught riding lessons to young girls. I spent mornings and afternoons at the stable, cleaning stalls, feeding horses, riding, and tending the animals. I took comfort in going back and forth to the barn.

Often, I dreamed that Joel would come home from work and announce that he was being transferred. Once, in a dream, he called me from Cleveland to say he had found a new house for us. Suddenly, I was wandering through the white halls of a large building, poking my head into doorways, asking, "Is this where I live?" People were sitting behind desks with old-fashioned typewriters on them. A woman with a pageboy haircut, who looked vaguely like me, raised her head as if she were startled but said nothing. I woke up anxious and irritable.

After eight years of living here, I have these dreams less frequently. I throw myself into activities for weeks, sometimes years. When people ask me what I do, I say I'm an editor, a horsewoman, or a writer. These titles offer a comfort I seem to need, a kind of anchor for my life. But sometimes I find myself feeling strangely out of sorts. I want to shrug out from under any semblance of identity. The routine that satisfied me for so long of going back and forth to the barn or writing each morning suddenly feels like drudgery. Perhaps on an unconscious level, I'm ready to move on, to pack up and leave. After all, it's my pattern, the only thing I know.

As a teenager I resented everything about Morehead City, mainly because it wasn't Panama. I hated the seasons and the way the cool wind swept off the sound. In Panama, we'd had five years of summer and I'd grown accustomed to it, learned to depend on it. Waiting for the bus on winter mornings in Morehead City, with my thin blood and summer clothes, I blamed North Carolina for my discomfort, my chattering teeth, and the headaches I got from the cold.

After my mother would come home from work, she'd lead me to the window, as if trying to show me there was beauty in this place. "There's nothing like watching the sun dip into the sound!" she'd say. "Just look at those colors."

It wasn't until I came back home to visit my parents with college friends and saw Morehead City through their eyes that I began to appreciate the sandy soil, the sapphire ocean, and the water-colored sunsets. North Carolina has grown on me, slowly and incrementally.

Recently, my sister moved to a town near Morehead City to be closer to my parents, who have moved into a rest home. Some days my sister and I meet at the sound or the beach. We sit and talk as the sky turns to peach, or we walk along the wet sand for miles as the salt air blows through our hair.

My brothers and I still gather at my parents' old house. Through the kitchen window, I see the blue-grey band of Bogue Sound and the white caps lacing its surface. Clouds look like cotton candy, palm trees, and ponies. Water mirrors the sky. The smallest details—like the shapes of trees crouching along the shore, the consistency of the air, or the exact color of the water when the sun hovers over it—have become a balm for my empty spaces. Each image or sensation is a fragment reflecting back a tiny piece of me. Each one leaves its impression, tells me I am home.

—*Ann Campanella*

Engine Run

Sitting at my desk in an old German bunker, I tried diligently to make sense of the previous secretary's notes: answering the phone, greeting commanding officers, reconciling the military spending accounts. It might as well have been written in hieroglyphics; the list of new acronyms alone was twenty pages thick.

Suddenly, a blast of noise reverberated through the building, steadily increasing in volume until it was so loud that I grabbed my keys and ran into the colonel's office. Expecting to see him opening the book *What to Do When They Push the Button*, I was floored to see him casually chatting on the phone with his boots on the desk. What was wrong with him? Or was it me? Was I going insane? Why wasn't he running for his helmet? Did he really not hear the thunderous apocalypse that was deafening me?

Noticing my panic, he hung up and walked toward me. I could see his lips move, but all I heard was a vibrating numbness at unbelievable decibels. I turned to run out the main door to the bunker. As I stepped into the street I was almost run over by a man on a Ducati motorcycle. The colonel grabbed my arm. He looked like a poorly timed mime, but I realized he was actually laughing. The noise started to wind down, like an old air raid siren, slowly deflating into nothing. Cutting through the noise like a jackhammer in mud, I heard the colonel's chuckles.

The colonel walked me out to the hangar off the tarmac, where he introduced me to Danny, the head C-20 mechanic. "This is Denise, our new secretary. She'd been on the job for all of three hours when the engine run practically sent her running to a rubber room. Why don't you walk her through the finer points while I go get her some ear plugs."

"Ma'am, nice to meet you," Danny said, taking off his helmet. "You oughta watch when you come out that door, ma'am; I nearly ran you over!"

Two "ma'ams" in less than thirty seconds; my skin crawled. I hated being called "ma'am." My new husband, Roger—a captain, who was already stationed at Ramstein Air Base in Germany when we married—had warned me that I'd have to get used to it, but whenever someone said "ma'am," I always looked around for my mother-in-law.

"Please call me 'Denise'," my voice oozed with politeness.

Danny gave me a pinched look that I have since come to realize means, "Not anytime soon."

Turning to look into the hangar, I caught sight of a huge metal scaffolding of sorts, holding an enormous engine.

"That is a C-20 engine off the colonel's plane." Danny's voice echoed in the massive hangar.

"Why is it here? Did something go wrong?" I asked.

"Not this one. Sometimes they are brought in for repairs, but usually it's just a scheduled maintenance." His voice sounded bored; he had told this too many times. "The engine is lowered onto the scaffolding out on the tarmac, then it's rolled away from the plane and into the hanger, where it is bolted to the floor."

"Why is it bolted to the floor?" I asked, immediately wishing I hadn't.

"Well, ma'am, we wouldn't want the engines getting away from us when it's time for the run," Danny explained, shaking his head a bit, as if he were talking to a simpleton. "Once it's bolted down, the mechanics take over. Each mechanic has highly honed skills, and they each have a specific task. No one mechanic is any less important than another; they each patiently support the engine and each other."

Now Danny was rambling, obviously in his element. "When they've finished their jobs, the engine is fired up and revved up to maximum RPM, physically sucking the air out of the room. The engine is run long and hard to test its strength and durability, to see whether it can handle speed and distance. Only after it has proven its endurance capability is it reattached to the airplane."

Danny looked at me to see if I was trailing or up to speed.

"Thanks, Danny, I appreciate the lesson" was all I could get out.

He actually tipped an invisible hat while saying ma'am this time, and I headed back to my office. On my desk was a pair of bright orange earplugs with a "Welcome to the Squadron" sticky on them.

I used that same sticky when Jenny, on her first base after completing boot camp, moved into the office next door. When the engine run began, she came careening into my office so pale I thought she'd faint on the spot. "Wh . . . wh . . . what is that?" she stammered, nearly screaming to be heard over the noise. I took her hand, sat her down, and waited until the run was over. Then I calmly gave her the explanation I had been given.

The engine run and accepting I was a ma'am were but two of the many adjustments I made during my first civilian job with the military—and they paled in comparison to the adjustments I've made as a military spouse.

Three years and three moves later, Roger brought up the idea of his deploying. Deployment: a deceptively benign word for a treacherous situation. My husband was being courteous, even respectful, by asking my opinion, but I knew he'd already made his decision. Roger and I are both from Colorado, and the Air Force offered to move us. So we decided that the kids and I would live there for the year Roger was deployed. Have you ever tried to convince a four-year-old that his bed will survive in the box? Well, we made it to Colorado, as did the bed, where we were surrounded by family and friends. We had our own personal crew of mechanics to make sure everything was a-okay on the home front and to help give us the strength to get through Roger's deployment.

Roger was there for two whole weeks before deploying. Since "home is where the Air Force sends us," he gently bolted us down in a house so small we had to put all of his things into storage. I was organizing the kids' clothes when I noticed our daughter, Sophia, sitting in her room, singing softly.

"Whatcha doing, Sophia?" I chirped to make her smile.

"Mommy, I sad." Her tiny two-year-old voice sounded hollow.

"Aw, honey, what's the matter?" My heart was tearing out of my chest.

"I want Daddy. Daddy gone. When Daddy home?" She said this with such emotion, I could tell she was really upset.

I grabbed a pillow off her bed and turned it so she could see the part with her daddy's face on it. All we had to remind us of our extraordinarily involved father and husband were a couple of pillows with his face on them and some photographs. It didn't seem like enough, and I realized we needed help.

I found a fantastic preschool for the kids, and I decided to find work, something to fill the time that normally Roger would. I found the right spot at the Airmen and Family Center on base.

On my way to Buckley Air Force Base, so nervous about my first day that I had cranked the air conditioning in the car higher than normal, I felt a tingling in my toes. I blew it off to nerves and pulled up to the gate. When I rolled down my window to show my ID, the heat of the day whacked me in the face. Then I heard it, a fantastic sound: F-16s doing touch-and-go's. Sucking in the jet exhaust, my lungs reacted as if it were like a breath of fresh air. I looked at the runway, and the next thing I knew, I had driven to the road at the end of the flight line and was sitting there crying. The sound of jets slicing through the clouds comforted me, a tonic for the heart.

Over the next few months, the vacuum blew up, the toaster caught fire, and the printer seized all the paper and part of the cat's tail. A few trips to Wal-Mart replaced those old, worn-out items. The first snow made me check my tires, which were shot. Luckily, there were several tire shops within a five-mile radius.

Dark spots showed up on a mammogram. Our military insurance provider, TRICARE, cancelled our prime enrollment because they thought I was in Iraq with Roger, and I found myself on the phone with some poor drone in a faraway land who told me that the double charge on my gas bill was because my meter hadn't been registering for over six months. I felt surrounded by unknown hands poking and fixing parts of my body and home.

Tyler and Sophia went to preschool, swim classes, play groups, and Grandma and Grandpa's house, surrounded by family and friends who did their best to meet their every need. Yet they were often feisty, cranky, or sullen. I worried that their childhood joy, their usual zest for life, and their curiosity were buried under the melancholy of missing their daddy. How could I find a mechanic to fix that?

One morning when I pulled into the preschool parking lot, the van shimmied. Yep, shimmied. I could not deal with yet another shimmy. Shushing the kids, I listened for a sign of complete internal failure. Nothing. Maybe it had just been the ice on the pavement.

I turned off the key, but the van continued to vibrate. Suddenly, Tyler's door flew open, and he bounded out into the parking lot and snow. He was screaming something, but I couldn't hear him. I struggled with Sophia's car seat while trying to keep Tyler's bobbing head and arms in view. Sophia was squirming and had started to sing. I couldn't figure out what was happening. Then I heard it, and how sweet it was. The F-16s swooped in their high-tech version of a dogfight right overhead. Tyler was cavorting in the parking lot, waving his arms over his head, screaming "Air Force! Hoo-ah! Air Force! Hoo-ah!" Sophia was dancing and singing her version of the Air Force theme song: "Nothing can stop the U and S force!"

I took a deep breath. I steadied my heart. We were home.

This deployment was our family's version of an engine run. We were separated from our body. Strapped down, we ran at top speed, and we were tested and graded on our endurance. We surrounded ourselves with people who fine-tuned us in some special way: the friend who helped revive us by taking us hiking in the mountains when it felt the air was sucked out of the room, grandparents who babysat so I could refuel, the schools that surrounded the children with safety, and a home to cool us down after a long hard run at the end of the day. At the end of the engine run, after we have proven ourselves, we will reattach and again soar into the clouds as one unit.

—Denise Neumann

Gung Ho

My fingers hovered above my keypad as the radio program I'd been listening to was interrupted by a special news report. It was just before noon, March 20, 2003, when the anxious voice of an embedded field reporter filtered across a continent and slithered into my office. I could barely make out his words over a high-pitched whine blaring in the background. He said he was in an amphibious assault vehicle. That he was on the move. Leaving the sands of Kuwait. Heading toward Baghdad.

My hands fell to my keys, and my eyelids dropped. It was happening. I knew without a doubt, at that precise moment, my son—a crewman on an amphibious assault vehicle—was also driving his track toward Baghdad. He was going to war. There was no stopping it. It had begun.

My fingers shook as I dialed the phone. I called the only other person who knew firsthand the sheer panic that shook me to the core. Another Marine mom. My sister.

"Melanie?"

"Sis."

"Melanie, they're moving. They're going in. It's too soon."

"I know, sis. I know," she whispered brokenly.

Words stuck in our throats. Unnatural silence stretched on. We couldn't talk. No words sufficed. We hung up without a goodbye. It was the shortest conversation of our adult lives.

Melanie's twenty-year-old Marine son, Lance, was a radio communications operator for his unit's captain. Lance and his beloved cousin—my nineteen-year-old son, Casey—were both in Kuwait. Both in the First Marine Division, in different companies. Both beginning the push to Baghdad.

Lance was six months older than Casey. They'd been inseparable since they were toddlers. Where Lance went, Casey followed. These two cousins shared a unique bond rarely witnessed. On the brink of manhood at the ages of sixteen and seventeen, they'd been sitting on a bench in the rain looking up at an American flag when they'd decided—right then and there—that they were both destined to be Marines.

They grew into men and never wavered from their convictions. They possessed a solid understanding of who they were, what they stood for, and where they were going. And they knew, beyond a doubt, why they were going to war and what they were fighting for.

We were a family of Marines. Melanie's middle son, Phil, was currently stationed in Okinawa, Japan. Our brother-in-law, Brian, was also a former Marine. Men seemed to accept war. For us women, it was incomprehensible. My mind would scream, No mother should ever have to send her son off to war! Then I would remember the wise words my son had spoken six months earlier.

"You know, Mom, when I was in boot camp I couldn't eat what I wanted, sleep when I wanted, or wear the clothes that I wanted. I couldn't listen to music or drive a car. I realized the Corps had taken away every freedom I had. And it became clear to me why I was there, why I've always wanted to be a Marine. It's to fight and protect my freedom. Because I now know what it's like not having it."

By the middle of August, both boys returned home from war. They took their post-deployment leave from Camp Pendleton and flew home to Indiana. Grandma and Grandpa Reese threw a welcome-home party. We ate, drank, and celebrated life.

A snapshot captured the faces of two battle-weary Marines, excited to be home, as they cut two yellow ribbons off a pear tree in the front yard.

February 2004 rolled around. I received a call from Casey around eight o'clock one evening. His unit was leaving in a month for their second tour, but he wasn't able to go. The sciatic nerve he'd been battling since Christmas turned out to be a herniated disk. He was having back surgery in two months. His buddies were leaving for Iraq without him. Bitter disappointment cut him like a knife.

Lance was gearing up to leave on his second tour the first of September 2004. His unit—the Second Battalion, Fifth Marines, Weapons Company—would be stationed at Hurricane Point in the city of Ar Ramadi, Al-Anbar Province, Iraq. He took his pre-deployment leave that July Fourth. Grandpa started up his grill, and the back yard was soon filled with family and fun. Lance skittered happily from one person to another, laughing, joking, living life to the fullest. He ended up next to his ninety-year-old great-grandmother's side.

"I hate to see you go, Lance," she said quietly.

"Grandma, don't worry. It's gonna be okay," he said, leaning in closely. "And you know what? If I don't make it back home, I know exactly where I'll be going."

And we all knew exactly what he meant. As he later told a buddy in Iraq, "I'll be walking with Jesus."

Lance and his brothers-in-arms were in our thoughts and prayers every hour of every day. His phone calls and letters sustained us:

Yeah, it does suck to hear that ya'll are having all this fun without me being there. But I'm enjoying what I'm doing out here, so it all makes up for it. I also get a great sense of pride because I know I'm making ya'll be able to do that.
—His response to missing out on a family reunion

I just wish I was with him to protect him, to guide him down the path on how to be a warrior.
—His comment to a girl cousin who was worried about her Marine boyfriend, who was soon to be deployed

I can't wait to get out of here. But I'm here. I'm going to do my job and do it well.
—A journal entry while on patrol in Ramadi

I love you. Have fun and be safe. STAY STRONG.
Semper Fi.
Love, Lance.

—His last letter home

Lance went to walk with Jesus on November 15, 2004. When he left this Earth, he took a piece of us with him. He left holes of various sizes in each one of us. But slowly, ever so slowly, his comforting spirit is filling those holes. Filling them with his smile. With happy memories. With the reality of his everlasting love.

Lance was gung ho about life and about his family, friends, and the Marine Corps. He proudly wore the gung-ho symbol tattooed on his inner left wrist. And now, so do his mother, two brothers, two aunts, one uncle, five cousins, and one future cousin-by-marriage. Each of us proudly displays the tattoo somewhere on our bodies, acknowledging to all that Lance will forever be a real part of our lives. Never to be forgotten.

Each and every one of us is Lance's immortality. Through us, Lance is alive.

—*Melinda Fay Stanley*

Debt of Honor

I am the wife, daughter, and granddaughter of Americans who have proudly served this country. Their legacy of military service has shaped and guided my life.

These three men I love are diverse in many ways, yet their love of country and their service to that country as veterans of foreign wars bind them together with a single thread of courage. They also share another common denominator: the unwritten code of silence about their experiences.

Though the sights and sounds of war are forever etched on a man's soul, they often remain buried deep within him. Memories too painful to recall, too horrific to share even with his soul mate, are stuffed into an internal box labeled "Keep Out." At night, when his guard is down, the scenes creep out and dance menacingly across the movie screen of his mind. The nightmares elicit restless nights, cold sweats, and silent screams. Sometimes, a scream escapes, waking the beloved sleeping by his side, but he quickly reassures her it was "just a nightmare" and leaves it at that. By day, he prays those nightmares stay locked in Pandora's box.

Such has been the case with my grandfather, father, and husband. The effects of war prey upon their minds and are etched upon their faces—a distinctive look that speaks of the unspeakable. Yet they rarely, if ever, share their ponderous burden even with those of us who would gladly shoulder it with them.

My husband and I met many years after his military service. Although I didn't experience sleepless nights worrying about Bill's safety or that he might not come home from war, I have lived daily with the consequences of those days long ago. Our relationship reflects the results of his service and sacrifice. When we first met, the connection sizzled across the room. Other guests felt the electricity in the air and saw the lightning flash between us. Two hearts wounded by the past were destined to find love that day. There was only one catch: Individually, we must surrender our pain, so together we could move forward. Although love had captured Bill's heart, the iron cage that kept it safe must be unlocked. Our future happiness was stronger than his haunting memories. It was time to step out in faith, letting love guide the way.

Fifteen years later, Bill's life prior to our meeting is still cloaked in mystery. Once in a great while, his emotions flirt with emerging but then quickly disappear, like a tortoise afraid to leave its shell. Our love is strong, yet the past still has a stranglehold on remote places of his heart.

After an illness nearly claimed Bill's life, we were offered a gift wrapped in an unusual package. Life presented us with the opportunity to give back to the community, including veterans who have bravely served our country. For more than ten years, my husband and I managed a low-income apartment community in the heart of the inner city. Many of our tenants were veterans, and they connected instantly with Bill.

To them, he became the officer in charge, without the commission, setting the tone for our tenure. Familiar military protocol brought relief to those who were unsettled and provided an environment where they could thrive and grow. When necessary, orders were barked out and followed without hesitation.

A bond formed not only between Bill and the veterans who lived in the building but also among those tenants, whose military service cut across time, rank, and branch. These relationships were genuine and often transparent. Whether Air Force, Army, Navy, Coast Guard, or Marine Corps, they all served as one to make our community safe and to keep the building clean.

There were no white-glove inspections, but their bunks were quarter-bouncing tight. Their living quarters could pass any inspection. Indeed, state building inspections were a breeze, as we gathered volunteers to assist in cleaning the common areas after they had cleaned their apartments. These events were reminiscent of past inspections under more hostile conditions. Although the inner city does have its share of drama and danger, a war zone still has the edge.

If trouble arose with an intruder or out-of-control tenant, there were men to cover our backs. More than once I remember facing danger, knowing that behind me was seamless support.

They had been well-trained, and it was a joy to have them as tenants.

Both men and women were eager to follow the rules and to meet our expectations. From young to old, their military backgrounds leveled the playing field. They shared a common mindset, a sense of unity, and a safe place to gather. Together, they relived distant memories that on some days seemed as if they had just occurred. The congenial but disciplined environment offered these brave but vulnerable soldiers the best of both worlds: security and freedom.

Just as their military service varied, so too did their personalities. And each encounter left an enduring memory in our hearts.

One vivid example was an older gentleman, a Vietnam War veteran, who could hear but whose speech was a casualty of war, an emotional injury that had rendered him selectively mute. He would communicate with Bill using hand gestures and signals common in military service. While I understood not a single word of their special sign language, they understood one another perfectly. This veteran also communicated with us via paper and pen, writing with beautiful penmanship that I envied.

As the days turned to weeks and then months, the relationship developed. Confidence and trust replaced inhibition and fear. The veteran began talking instead of signaling or writing his message. At first he spoke little and haltingly, but as time went on and the conversations grew, his verbal skills improved. Eventually, he started speaking to me and then to other tenants whom he trusted. Respect, patience, and acceptance had wooed him from the dark place where he had hidden himself for years.

Then his health began to fail. Soon, he would need more support than we could offer. In the meantime, though, he was in a safe place, where he was accepted for who he was and recognized for what he had done.

Within the environment we created, other veterans also grew in confidence. They healed, both physically and emotionally. Some mended broken relationships and reunited with loved ones.

Did we help them all? No, though not because we did not try our best. Some remain trapped in a place far across the sea, their minds held hostage by an enemy that had ravaged their souls long ago and had stolen their friends and bunkmates, their peace and often their innocence.

The experience was not without its cost. As community leaders, we often observed and absorbed the impact of those encounters with the past. As amazing as it is to witness healing, it is equally devastating when efforts fail to help and the results are catastrophic.

My husband experienced many moments of accomplishment and joy. Other days, the weight of grief and stress drove his blood pressure higher. After more than a decade, we left that community. It was a difficult decision to leave behind what we had built, but it wasn't worth dying for. The price Bill was paying for serving the survivors was similar to the price he'd paid long ago serving his country.

So, together, we move on. The future pages of our journey are still unwritten. But one thing I know for sure is that my husband will remain a military man at heart and in his soul for all of his days, just like my father and grandfather.

Three generations. Three wars. One common denominator: love, loyalty, and proud service to their country.

My grandfather, my father, and my husband each paid a high price so that I could live in a free country today. Daily, proudly, I strive to repay their debt of honor.

—*Barbara J. Hollace*

The Backup Plan

My friend Kristi placed both hands over her maternity smock and frowned.

"Are you okay?" I asked.

"I had a contraction, but it didn't hurt. It was probably just a Braxton Hicks." She patted her protruding belly. "Maybe I'd better sit down."

Kristi waddled over to a park bench, and I pushed our kids on the toddler swings while we waited for another contraction. None came, but the false alarm had scared us. The baby wasn't due for another three weeks.

"If I go into labor before my parents get here, will you take me to the naval hospital?" she asked.

I hesitated before answering. The only experience I'd had in a hospital was when I'd given birth to my son, a memory clouded by pain. "Do you mean drive you there or stay with you the whole time?"

A look of disappointment flashed across her face. She shrugged. "As much as you want to do."

Immediately I felt badly about hesitating and dissecting her question. She shouldn't have to go through labor alone. If I were eight months pregnant and my husband was out to sea, I'd want someone there with me through the entire birth.

"I'll stay with you until you have the baby," I promised.

But I was actually thinking, *Your mother will be coming soon, and she'll help you through labor. I'm just the backup plan.*

Of all the hardships Navy life deals us—frequent moves, living away from extended families, long separations from our mates—separations are the worst. And of all the special times to be separated from our husbands—birthdays, anniversaries, holidays—the birth of a baby has to be the hardest. I'd been lucky to have Mark with me when our son was born, but since he'd been transferred to the submarine base in Groton, Connecticut, he'd been gone more than he'd been home. Sometimes his boat was deployed for five months at a time. Rather than go through pregnancy and childbirth without my spouse, I'd decided not to have any more children.

Kristi, however, didn't want her daughter, Holly, to be an only child. She'd set her sights on having a boy with red hair and freckles, just like her husband. Greg's submarine was on a regular three-month-in, three-month-out schedule, but despite careful planning, the baby was going to be born while Greg's sub was on patrol somewhere in the middle of the ocean.

I phoned Kristi often to check up on her. On sunny days we took our kids to the petting zoo or walked around the park and chatted. We were both glad to have someone to talk with who wasn't two years old. Kristi and I joked that, although our men weren't stationed on the same submarine, the two of us were in the same boat.

Kristi had a few more Braxton Hicks contractions, and each time I wondered, *Am I going to be the one taking her to the hospital? Will I know what to do? What if I panic or pass out? Maybe I'll be so caught up in my own emotions I won't support her enough.*

I was very relieved the day her parents flew in from Texas. They hovered around her, watching for any sign of impending labor, but nothing happened.

"He's waiting for his daddy to come home," Kristi's mother said.

After a week, Mrs. Davidson reluctantly returned to her job in Texas. Kristi's father stayed behind; he had recently retired and so could remain as long as needed.

Now that Kristi's mother was out of the picture, Mr. Davidson would be taking Kristi to the hospital and helping her when his grandchild was born. I volunteered to babysit Holly any time of the day or night, a job that was originally going to be his.

Mr. Davidson thanked me for my offer. Then he remarked with a nervous laugh, "Unless you want to go with Kristi, and I'll stay home with the kids."

I got the impression that he was as squeamish about going to the hospital as I was. He told me he'd been in the service himself and had missed both his children's births. I suspected that, even if he'd been available, he would have waited outside the delivery room, like most men of that time.

My radar must have been accurate. One afternoon the phone rang and Kristi's frantic voice blurted out, "I'm having contractions, and my father's not here!"

"Where is he?" I asked.

"He was bored and drove up to Massachusetts to buy Matchbox cars for his collection."

"Bored?" I said in disbelief. How could he have left her when she was past her due date? "When do you expect him back?"

"Probably not until late tonight."

"Hold on! I'll be there as soon as I can."

I strapped my son into his car seat and sped off in the direction of Kristi's. When I arrived, Kristi and Holly were sitting on their front step.

"How are you doing?" I asked.

"The contractions are coming about every five minutes."

"Good," I said. "We have plenty of time."

I rushed her to the car, anyway, carrying the suitcase and opening the door for her, all the while feeling like a poor substitute for Greg.

Kristi was feeling her husband's absence, too. "Greg's missing the baby's birth by only ten days," she moaned. My heart went out to her.

After dropping off the kids with my neighbor in military housing, I took Kristi to the base hospital and escorted her inside. Everything up to that point had happened so fast that I hadn't had a chance to think. But once we were inside the hospital, time slowed down.

I was allowed to stay with Kristi after she was admitted. At first, I cringed when she was in pain. But Kristi was a trooper, panting and blowing with each contraction. Still, I worried, *Do I remember enough Lamaze breathing to coach her when things get rough?* We hadn't gone to classes together and had never rehearsed. I was only supposed to be the backup plan. It occurred to me that, with all the time we spent together, we could have practiced once or twice, just in case.

A nurse rolled in the fetal monitor. She gently attached an elastic band around the hump on my friend's abdomen, then smeared jelly on two discs and placed them underneath the band. When she turned on the machine, it started beeping in time with the baby's heartbeat.

"Your baby is fine," the nurse said to Kristi, and we were both reassured.

Two pens made scratching noises as they etched zigzags on a long strip of graph paper that chugged out of the machine, folding like a fan when it hit the floor. The nurse studied the paper.

"Here comes another contraction," she said.

Kristi winced and brushed away a strand of hair.

"Shallow breaths," I reminded her, but midway through she lost her focus and whimpered. "Pant!" I said. "Try to stay in control."

Kristi panted until the contraction peaked, but then she lost her concentration again.

"Now blow!" I said.

Her lips formed a circle, and she blew and blew. When the contraction subsided, she let out a sigh. I handed her a cup of ice chips.

"I left a note on the kitchen counter for my father," she said, sucking on a piece of ice. "Maybe he didn't see it. Could you try calling the house?"

"Sure." I went to the nurses' station to use the phone. Mr. Davidson had not gotten back yet, so I left a message on the answering machine.

Kristi had wanted an all-natural birth, but after six hours she was losing stamina and her back hurt. The nurse reached behind Kristi into the opening of her gown and rubbed the small of her back. Kristi took deep breaths and slowly relaxed.

When the contractions started coming closer and closer together, the nurse stretched on Latex gloves to check Kristi's progress. "You're fully dilated," she said. "I'll tell the midwife."

When she returned, she handed me a faded green gown, a mask, and a head covering that looked like a shower cap. I put the gown on over my sweater, stuffed my long hair inside the cap, and tied on the mask. I kept expecting Mr. Davidson to show up at any second and take my place, but he was nowhere to be seen. The nurse released the brake on the bed, and I helped her roll it down the hall. *Here we go,* I thought, excitement flowing through me. The warm air I exhaled into my mask fogged my glasses, which made everything seem surreal.

We entered the delivery room, and the nurse propped Kristi up with pillows and helped her get her feet into the stirrups. The nurse stood on one side of her, and I stood on the other. Every time Kristi had a contraction, we gently moved her shoulders forward. The contractions were coming one on top of another now.

"Can you see?" the midwife asked me.

She tilted a round mirror down, and I nodded. The baby's head was crowning.

Two more contractions, and the head popped out.

"Okay, I want you to give me one more big push," the midwife said.

Kristi bent forward and reached for the bed rail, but I grabbed her hand in midair and she gripped my fingers tightly. She grunted, screaming only once, and the shoulders gradually emerged. Finally, a waxy-looking baby slid out, face down, into the midwife's hands. She suctioned the nose and mouth, and the baby began to squall. The midwife held her up for us to see, and we four women shared a wonderful moment as we witnessed this perfect, healthy baby taking her first breaths.

"A girl," Kristi said with a smile. "Another girl."

Though masks covered the other women's faces, the wrinkles at the corners of their eyes told me they were smiling too. So was I. For a fleeting moment, I wished I were Kristi and the baby girl was mine.

The midwife clamped the rubbery umbilical cord and laid the infant on Kristi's abdomen. "Shhh," Kristi whispered.

That night, I picked up the kids from my neighbor's, took them home, gave them baths, and put them to bed. Soon after they fell asleep, the phone rang. Mr. Davidson had just returned to Kristi's house, found the note she'd left, and listened to my message on the answering machine. I told him Holly was welcome to stay the night and that if he left for the hospital now, he could see Kristi before visiting hours were over.

"Thank you for helping my daughter," he said. "I'm so glad she and the baby are all right."

I think the poor man was even happier the ordeal was over and he was off the hook. How he knew what day to disappear would always be a mystery to me.

Kristi and I shared many experiences while our husbands were stationed on submarines, but the birth of her baby is one I'm sure I will never forget. That day the phrase "extended family" took on a whole new meaning as I realized that I was part of a sisterhood of Navy wives who helped each other through difficult times. Our men couldn't always be there for us, but we would always be there for each other. I didn't feel so alone anymore . . . and I reconsidered my decision not to have another child. Today, I have a beautiful daughter of my own.

—*Mary Laufer*

A Little Girl and a Big War

When I was small, my father and I would walk our collie around the junior high school near our house in rural Pennsylvania. I was less than three feet tall, and my father was a hint over six feet. He had been among the first drafted to serve in World War II, and he liked to play army with me.

"Left. Right. Left. We had a good home, and we left," he called over the grounds of the school.

I would march next to him, tucking in my tummy and keeping my head upright, exhibiting what I hoped was perfect U.S. Army posture, while the dog ignored us completely as he sniffed peonies and for-sythia bushes. The three of us would make it around the ten acres of the school this way. Every so often we would run into another person walking a dog, but we never broke rank; instead, we preferred to salute the civilian/canine and march straight ahead.

When we left the school property, we would return to our father/daughter status—our shoulders and chins relaxed, the dog back on its leash. Then my father would begin a soliloquy about his time in Patton's Third Army, remembering friends who had died and those who had survived. Sometimes he would tear up, and then I would, too.

One day I asked him why he talked about the war so much.

"I spent five years of my youth in the Army," he said. "A very critical five years."

I remember thinking, *His youth? Why, he was twenty-five when he was drafted!*

The summer I was eight we vacationed in France. My father wanted to recreate the Battle of the Bulge with me. Together, with my mother in tow, we traveled to one small French town after another, bingeing on stinky cheese and soft baguettes, while reliving war strategies, bombings, and mostly losses. At times, even though I knew the Americans were ultimately victorious, I could not envision Hitler losing. It didn't seem possible; according to Dad, it wouldn't have been without General Patton.

"Patton taught us to care about every single American soldier. He taught us to value every single American life. Best of all, he knew how to win a battle."

One day after many years of dodging questions that I tossed like bullets, he told me what it had been like to liberate Buchenwald, the concentration and work camp outside of Weimar, Germany.

"We didn't want to go in," he acknowledged truthfully.

"The Germans were losing and were trying to kill everyone they could before they officially declared defeat. Snipers were everywhere. We were a detached unit, so Patton called us and we were among the first to enter.

"When we arrived at the camp, we couldn't believe what we found. I ordered my men back out to our tents to get their cameras. We needed photographs. We needed documentation. I didn't think anyone would ever believe what we found there."

My dad's concentration camp photographs predate most others, including those of *LIFE* magazine and famed photographer Margaret Bourke White.

Eisenhower believed strongly in military personnel taking photographs of the war effort; it was sanctioned. That's why World War II is so well documented.

Long before he was in the Army, my dad loved taking pictures. So later, when he joined the Army Corps of Engineers, he took photos of everything.

But the photographs of Buchenwald are difficult to look at. Dead people were piled up like hundreds of Idaho potatoes. My father could hardly look at them. He hated to remember that place.

"It stunk of death," he would say, his eyes welling up.

Though he spent only four days there, he had nightmares about it for the rest of his life.

One day after school, while I was dunking a half dozen Oreos into a half gallon of milk, my mom turned on *The Mike Douglas Show*. He had a concentration camp survivor as his guest. We watched, riveted to our black-and-white television. The survivor told of the horrors, the inhumanities, and finally, the liberation of Buchenwald.

Then she said, "I would like to thank Major Saxer. I never got to thank him."

My mother and I couldn't believe it! This woman had just thanked Dad on television. We couldn't wait to tell him when he came home from work that night. I let Mom spill the beans. My father did not say a word; his face remained oddly still. Finally, he nodded and put his head down on the table.

After a few moments, he composed himself and pulled me into his chest for a big bear hug. My mother placed her hand on his shoulder, and the three of us held each other.

I asked Dad if he was okay.

Smiling slightly, he said, "Yes. I'm very lucky to be here." Then, like the soldier he had been, he pulled himself up ramrod straight and, left to change his clothes.

My mother pulled me into the kitchen. "He doesn't want to talk about it," she whispered. "Let's make dinner. Why don't you set the table?"

With that, the subject was closed . . . until some other day when my dad and I would again walk the dog over to the junior high, fall into rank, short behind tall, and march.

—Melanie Saxer Johnston

For Every Tear, a Smile

The first time my husband was deployed, we had been married only four months and I was still adjusting to having left my family and the area where I'd grown up to move 1,200 miles away to Fort Polk, Louisiana. Although moving from a big city that had been home all my life to a small town where nothing was familiar was traumatic, I decided to make the best of our time there.

At twenty-four, I was young and able-bodied and not the stay-at-home type, so within three weeks of being in Louisiana I landed a job at a local veterinary clinic. I enjoyed it very much, and just as I was getting used to my new routine and new "home," I got the news that my husband, Richard, was leaving for Afghanistan.

By then, two months after arriving in Louisiana, I'd managed to make a few new friends, meet my new neighbors, and adjust to my new surroundings. And it all suited me just fine . . . until I realized I'd soon be alone in a place where everything was new. These virtual strangers in a strange state, miles from home and from comfort, were all I had. There was no one who really knew me, no one I could confide in.

The day my husband deployed, I bore it all alone. I tried to hold it together in front of neighbors, but I was honestly frightened and lonely. It just wasn't the same there without him.

Two days after my husband left, my cell phone rang while I was at work. I didn't recognize the number. It was my husband! I was so happy to hear his voice, and I ran outside so we could talk privately. All too soon, our allotted ten-minute conversation was over and we were cut off. I began to weep hysterically as my mind raced: *What was I doing here? Why did my husband have to go? Why did it have to happen so close to the holidays?*

I forced myself to calm down. I quickly wiped away my tears and went back into the clinic, lowering my head to hide my tear-stained cheeks and reddened eyes. In the bathroom, I washed my face and tried to pull myself together.

When I returned to my station at the front desk, a woman was standing there holding one small child in her arms and the hand of another slightly older child at her side. Locking her eyes on mine, she explained that one of my coworkers had told her my husband was deploying.

"Is this your first time, hon?" she asked.

I told her it was.

"How long have you-all been married?" she asked.

"Almost five months, ma'am," I replied.

I finished up with her bill, ashamed that my face was still red and that her questions were making me want to cry again.

As she was walking out the door with her small brood, she turned to me and said, "Thank you, dear."

"You're welcome," I said and turned to finish the tasks at hand.

"No," she said. "I mean, thank you for your sacrifice. My husband got to come home to have Christmas with his wife and children because women like you send their husbands to relieve other men. No one is more thankful or more aware of the sacrifices you make than someone who has made the same ones. So, from one Army wife to another, thank you, sister. Thank you."

With that, she turned and left, leaving me speechless.

I don't recall ever seeing her again. But knowing that my husband's absence meant another family could create happy Christmas memories together made that day and every day after a little easier for me to get through.

—*Lauren M. Turner*

Welcome Home

On a lovely Midwestern spring day in April 1969, I reached expectantly for the ringing telephone and smiled when I heard my husband's voice. Walt was an airman stationed at Scott Air Force Base, Illinois, where I also worked as a civilian clerk-stenographer.

"Hi, honey. Guess what?" I tried to contain my excitement.

"What did the doctor say?" Walt got right to the point.

I held the phone close and whispered so only he would hear, wanting him to be the first to learn our good news. "We're going to have a baby in November."

Silence on the other end.

"Aren't you happy?" I asked.

"Sure, I'm happy. But . . ."

"But what?"

"I got orders today."

My throat tightened. My voice grew shrill. "Orders? For where?"

"Tan Son Nhut. In August." He paused. "I'm excited about the baby, but I gotta go. We'll talk tonight."

My hands shook as I hung up. Evelyn, our office secretary, put an arm around me and asked what was wrong. For a few minutes I couldn't speak, then I blurted the news about my pregnancy and Walt's orders. Soon I was surrounded by coworkers. I sobbed uncontrollably. At the sight of my tears, the pilots in the office turned on their heels and scuttled back to their desks, as if they were under attack. Evelyn led me to the restroom.

During the months that followed I discovered the meaning of being part of the "military family." My boss, an Air Force major, generously granted me time off for doctor's visits, and he didn't complain when bouts of morning sickness kept me from work. A few of the pilots stopped smoking cigars when they noticed that I had to run to the restroom whenever they lit up.

One of the nicest surprises was my baby shower. Even the men participated. When Walt picked me up afterward, our car was filled with baby clothes, a bassinet, a changing table, and diapers. There was even a card with money.

Our most treasured gift, though, was the delay of Walt's deployment until January. He would still be shipped to the war zone, but his duty station was changed to a safer destination, Cam Ranh Bay, and he would be with me for the birth of our first child.

On November 14, we were delighted when our beautiful baby girl, Julie, was born. After the Christmas holidays, all three of us moved in with my family in Missouri. Walt and I tried to make the most of our time together before he left.

The inevitable occurred on a frigid Saturday in late January. In St. Louis's Lambert Airport, I cradled Julie and watched Walt disappear into a plane that would carry him off to war.

Time crept by. Nightly news reports showing body counts didn't help. Six days a week I raced to the mailbox, looking for a thin blue envelope with Walt's letter inside. My dad, a World War II combat veteran, assured me that because Walt was a "rear echelon commando" (the name Dad called anyone in the Air Force), he would be safe.

"Now, if he were Army Infantry, like I was, you might have something to worry about," Dad joked.

Caring for Julie kept me busy and gave me joy. Her first word was "dada," which I promptly taped and sent to Walt.

Some Saturdays Walt was able to call home by way of ham radio. Those evenings, I sat in the kitchen praying for the phone to ring. My pulse would race when the operator said, "Hold the line for a call from Vietnam." Our calls were limited to a few minutes of conversation that went like this:

"I love you. Over."

"I love you, too. I miss you and Julie. Over."

Not very romantic, but the sound of his voice on those lonely Saturday nights helped me to persevere.

While Walt was overseas, my brother Jimmy got drafted. After he left for basic training at Fort Leonard Wood, life at home became even more stressful.

One Friday evening, I sat in the living room playing with Julie. I glimpsed two men in uniform walk up the sidewalk. Fearing the worst, I grabbed Julie and ran into the bedroom. I reasoned that if I didn't hear the words, it wouldn't be real.

Shortly afterward, Mom knocked on the door. "Donna, can you come out for a minute?"

I didn't answer.

She persisted. "Come on out. Jimmy's here with one of his Army friends."

Red-faced, but relieved the men in uniform weren't Air Force messengers bearing bad news, I hugged my little brother.

On another cold night in January, Walt returned home. He walked off the plane, tan and handsome in his Air Force blues. No parades or crowds welcomed him home, just Julie and me. I ran into his arms, while Julie skipped through the airport, yelling, "Daddy! Daddy!" I thanked God Walt was safe and soon to be a civilian.

But all was not cheery in our world.

Shortly before Walt left for Vietnam, his mother had been diagnosed with cancer. By the end of his tour, her condition had worsened. Fortunately, after his discharge, we moved to Massachusetts and found comfort spending time with his mom before she passed.

In 1972, we were thrilled to be expecting our second child. Then one late spring day the phone rang.

After asking how I felt, Dad cleared his throat. "I have some news," he said. "I wanted to tell you before one of your friends called or you read about it in the paper."

"What are you talking about, Dad?"

"Remember the Blassie boy? The one who took you to your prom?"

"Sure. Why?"

In a somber voice Dad told me that Mike's plane had been shot down. He was classified as "killed in action, body not recovered."

After hanging up, I prayed for Mike and remembered my senior prom, just six years earlier. At the all-girls' high school I'd attended in St. Louis, the girls invited the boys to prom. Mike was a senior at an all-boys' school. I didn't know Mike very well but had developed a crush on him after seeing him at church and watching him play tennis at a local park. Hoping for the best, I invited him, and to my surprise, he accepted. That special night, Mike's voice filled with pride when he told me he'd been accepted into the Air Force Academy. I remember how grown-up I felt when he kissed me goodnight on the front porch. Shortly after graduation, my family moved to the suburbs, and Mike left for Colorado. I never saw him again.

In October 1972, I gave birth to my son, Walter Erik. That same month, human remains were recovered from a crash site in Vietnam. The remains were "believed to be" Mike's but were designated "unknown."

Twenty-six years later, in early 1998, Walt and I were back living in Missouri. Julie and Erik were young adults; the Vietnam War was a distant memory. Early one morning, the phone rang. It was my sister, Kathleen.

"Turn on Channel Four," she said.

"Why?"

"They think they can identify the Vietnam veteran buried in the Tomb of the Unknown Soldier."

"The what?"

"The Unknown Soldier," Kathleen said. "They think it's Mike Blassie."

For days, television stations flashed photos of Mike—in his uniform, with his family, in his pilot's suit next to a jet. I dug my prom pictures out from the cedar chest and reminisced.

In a snapshot my mom had taken, under the watchful eye of my father and the shy smile of my baby sister, Bridget, Mike pinned a corsage on the yellow-and-white formal I had borrowed from a friend. In another photo, I stood tall with angel curls stacked atop my head, and Mike stood next to me wearing a dark suit with a white boutonniere pinned to the lapel. He had one arm around my waist, one hand touching my white-gloved arm. We smiled and stared straight ahead—standing on the edge of our futures, gazing into the vast unknown.

I waited until the media furor died down before calling Mike's mom, Jean. After introducing myself, I asked if she would like copies of the pictures.

"Yes. Thank you," she said quietly.

During our conversation she told me that the Defense Department was still trying to determine if the remains were definitely Mike's. How difficult that must've been for her.

In May 1998, the Pentagon announced DNA tests confirmed that the remains in the Tomb of the Unknown Soldier were those of First Lieutenant Michael Joseph Blassie. His family requested he be returned to St. Louis for burial. A month later, the Blassie family sent me an invitation to the interment ceremony.

On a cloudy day in July, Walt and I drove to Jefferson Barracks National Cemetery. As we approached the manicured grounds, I was moved by the respectful crowd standing watch. Near the gravesite, Walt and I were ushered to a roped-off area, where we watched Mike's flag-draped casket arrive with an honor guard. The Secretary of Defense, local senators and dignitaries, and the St. Louis Archbishop stood front and center with the Blassie family. The burial ceremony was dignified and honorable; the music touching. I choked back tears when an Air Force missing-man formation flew overhead.

In the receiving line, Mrs. Blassie thanked me again for the photos. I introduced Walt and told her he also had served in the Air Force in Vietnam. As I continued through the line, I noticed Mrs. Blassie hug Walt and say something to him.

We left shortly after paying our respects. Walt had a faraway look, and I asked if he was okay.

"Yeah," he said. "Today is the first time that has happened to me."

"What?" I asked.

"Mrs. Blassie said something that, outside of family and friends, no one else has ever said."

"What did she say?"

"Welcome home."

As we drove home in a comfortable silence, a gentle rain began to fall, and my spirit was soothed by this thought: On that rainy day in July, decades after the last drop of American blood had been shed in Vietnam, another veteran—who was, indeed, known and loved by many—had finally come home.

—*Donna Duly Volkenannt*

When Dad Leaves for War: Connor's Story

When Dad picks me up from school today, he says he has some news.

"Are we going to Blockbuster today to pick out a new video game?" I asked with my new tooth-missing grin.

"Not quite what I had in mind, Connor, but maybe we can go later," Dad says in his matter-of-fact voice. "Did you have a good day in school today? Did you get another apple?"

"I sure did. Do you want to see it?" I ask, and then giggle excitedly.

"Good job!" he tells me while checking out my apple and grinning.

"Did you know I'm working at sitting still and using my ears more than my mouth at circle time? Because in first grade, Dad, that is a really big deal, and Grammy, said before we know it, I will have a whole orchard on our refrigerator!"

"Your Grammy is one smart lady, and she knows you very well. She also has room for her own apple orchard on her refrigerator once ours is full."

After fixing my seat belt nice and snug, Dad jumps into his seat, buckles up, and quickly starts up our really cool dual-exhaust truck. While waiting to go, he gets quiet for a moment like he's thinking about something and quickly wipes something from his eyes before putting on his new blue reflective cop sunglasses. Then as he checks himself out in the rearview mirror, he looks at me in the back seat and his smile escapes.

Finally, he remembers to turn on the tunes, and I watch as he picks out our favorite country CD. Now with the familiar sounds of our song, "I Want to Be Just Like You, Dad," blaring, we start singing together with the windows down on this warm winter day, riding home in our big shiny blue truck.

What's this? Dad just drove right past our street; he must have decided to go to Blockbuster's after thinking about the new Xbox 360 display for a minute or two. I'm so glad I thought of it first! All of a sudden he pulls into our favorite parking spot at Burger King near Grammy's work. Now I begin to wonder: It isn't karate night or haircuts at Barber Tom's, so why is Dad taking me to get a Happy Meal in the afternoon? What if my appetite gets ruined? Mom is going to be mad. . . . But as I jump from the truck, I notice they are giving out a new toy that I need to get. Mom would understand our burger stop. She knows how cool a new prize is, and besides, I always give Dad my fries to eat so later I don't get a stomachache.

After picking out the best seat in the place for Dad and me, I anxiously start to unwrap my new toy while stuffing my mouth with my cheeseburger and notice my dad bowing his head to thank God for our meal. So I put down my almost-opened new treasure and fold my hands together to say grace. I hear my dad pray to God to keep me and Mom and Shane safe while he is deployed.

I ask him what deployed means. Is it a new game? It sounded like the Battleship Game that I always beat Grammy at on Webkinz.

"Don't you ever let the old lady win?" he laughs. Then he says he just realized how important Grammy and Webkinz will be to me while he is away . . . downrange. He explains that along with the guys at the base, he'll be going away for a few months to help other soldiers while they rebuild a country and help put an end to the war.

While I proudly hold up my new lime green I-Dog I say, "But Auntie Ashley and Uncle Matt are already winning the war! With Auntie in her Blackhawk and

Uncle Matt's tanks, they will have it done in a few days, Dad, so now you can stay home with me. Besides, who will drive your police cruiser around keeping our streets safe? How will we get money for our bills, if you are not working another road job or staying late like you always do, working a double? Who will take care of me and my brother when Mom is at work? Who will take me to school in the morning and pick me up every day like you always do?

"I was just getting good at The Game of Life that Santa got me for Christmas. I like to play with you every night just before bed; it would take me a million years to teach Grammy all the rules. What about our haircuts at Barber Tom's? Mom can't take me; you know the rules—no girls allowed.

"What about our puppy, Buddy? You're the only one Mom lets him sleep with. What about my karate class? Don't you want to see me get my orange belt? You will be disappointed, Dad, if you're not there. What about our bike rides to Stanley Park? It won't be the same at the swings without you pumping right next to me!

"I don't think this deploy-on-range sounds like a very good idea. Maybe they could get some cowboys and Indians to go instead of you; they know how to ride horses and they are good at fighting and they always come with guns in their hands! Dad, isn't that a good idea? Then you won't miss my birthday party and our pool and going to the Cape with Auntie and Emma. No one will be here to help me stop the ice cream man all summer. . . ."

I stop and catch my breath. My bottom lip starts to quiver while I bravely wipe away the tears spilling onto my cheeks.

After finishing our lunch and helping my dad clean up, we walk hand-in-hand back to the truck. All the while, he says I have very good reasons for his not leaving. He cannot believe how fast I'm growing up and how I seem to notice everything. He tells me that because I am so smart at six years old, I will be all right. I'll understand that there are people and many young children living in Iraq in burnt-down houses without any clean water to drink or enough food to eat or even schools for the children to go to safely.

"Without a car, the family must walk everywhere, and some of the children don't even own a warm jacket or a decent pair of shoes." I hear the pride in his voice as he explains that he must go to do his part to help fight the War on Terror; this is what the Air Force has trained him to do.

As we drive home, he tells me that everything is all worked out and that Mom will not be going to work while he is away. She will be dropping me off and picking me up from school every day, and she will also be taking me to karate class. She would even make an exception to continue our burger-and-prize routine afterward, even though Burger King is not her favorite.

He reminds me that she always makes a video of my belt ceremonies, only this time she will make two copies and send one of them to him in Iraq to see. He says Grampy or Will can take me to Barber Tom's for my haircuts and that it will be just as much fun to ride bikes with Mom and Shane, or even Grammy, all the way to the swings and Shane's trails at Stanley Park.

As we pull into our driveway, he tells me I will still go to the Cape like we do every year, and the water in my pool will continue to be refreshing and crystal-clear.

"While I am away, I would like you to be in charge of taking care of Buddy every day. You will need to feed him and walk him and, most important, from now on he gets to sleep with you in your bed every night."

As we walk through the door into the warmth of our home and the smells of Mom cooking dinner at the stove and Shane painting his models up in his room, I start feeling that good-to-be-home feeling in my stomach again. My dad picks me up and hugs me real tight, while he asks me if I understand that he will be back home soon and everything will be all right while he is away.

Then, in a serious voice before putting me down, Dad says, "But Connor, there is one more thing. As far as chasing down the ice cream truck, you and your older brother, Shane, are on your own."

Later that night, as I'm drifting off to sleep, I decide I can deal with a little less ice cream in my six-year-old life. This deployment will be like when my dad is working a double or is at a road job on his Guard weekend, like he always does. Mom will take good care of me and my brother the way only my mom knows how to do, and I may get to spend every weekend at Grammy and Grampy's house. That would be great! I really like hanging out in camo, watching fishing and hunting on television with my Grampy all of the time. Best of all, sleeping right beside me, under my covers, will be my puppy, my little Buddy.

As I fold my hands to talk to God, I ask him to watch over my dad and my Auntie Ashley and Uncle Matt, who are playing cowboys and Indians and riding horses in Iraq. I then ask God to send some clean water and food, if he has enough, and to try to find some warm jackets and new school shoes for all the kids in Iraq. He could buy lots of them at Wal-Mart; they always have plenty. I let God know I'm going to be okay while my dad is away working a road job and staying late for a double, keeping the streets safe for all the kids walking to school in Iraq.

—*Linda M. Powers*

Advice for a New Marine

I am sitting in a window seat on a flight from Atlanta to Rochester when I notice a family boarding the plane, all wearing green Marine Corps sweatshirts. I know what that means. After the mother and daughter settle into the row kitty-corner from me, I ask if they have just attended graduation.

"Yes," exclaims the mother. "We had nine people in attendance."

A young man with a fresh high-and-tight haircut boards the plane, and I ask him if he is the new Marine.

"Yes, ma'am," he answers.

I congratulate him, and he beams, happy for the recognition, happy to have survived the drill instructors, happy to be heading home.

It brings back memories of when my son, Nick, graduated from boot camp in November 2004, one of the signature events in both of our lives. Nick had been a lazy, slovenly teenager who barely passed his courses because he just didn't care about school. He had one desire: to be a Marine. He signed his enlistment papers on his seventeenth birthday, then waited almost a full year to leave for boot camp. He departed in droopy jeans and baggy T-shirt in the company of a staff sergeant in crisp dress blues. It seemed a far stretch that in three months he'd resemble the recruiter more than his old self, but on graduation day, he stood ramrod straight, tanned and strong, in the crisp day uniform of the United States Marines.

It's difficult enough for any parent when a child leaves home, but to be the parent of a young recruit is a test of faith and endurance. I remember listening to the mother of a young woman who had just headed to college complain about the number of times her daughter called each day. While Nick was at boot camp, I went thirteen weeks without hearing my firstborn's voice. Our only communication was letters. I wrote to him almost daily, and he wrote home once a week; his scratching on the page became a Wednesday challenge to decode. I knew he would be okay, but still I checked the mail anxiously to keep watch on how he was progressing. He was where he wanted to be, and I wanted that for him, too, but I missed being part of his life, and I missed him in mine.

With my parents, I drove to South Carolina for Nick's graduation. It was my father's first time back at Parris Island since he had been a brash, young recruit in 1948. I was thrilled for him, but I had come for one thing: to see my son become a Marine. On the afternoon before graduation day, we watched rehearsal. I had trouble picking Nick out of the formation—they all looked alike—so Dad handed me his old binoculars.

"Straight ahead, third from the end."

I focused the lenses, and as Nick came into view, I felt the air leave my lungs. Dad asked, "Can you see him?" but I could not answer. My boy was as completely beautiful, as absolutely perfect, as the first time I'd seen him in the moments after his birth. Now, Nick standing at ease, tanned and muscular, but so small in his cammies and wearing incredibly nerdy government-issued glasses. I took a breath and then another, and when I could breathe evenly, I handed the binoculars back to Dad and smiled.

"Bet he loves those glasses."

It took an hour of practice until the drill instructors were satisfied with the recruits' performance. Our rear ends had gone numb sitting on the metal bleachers, but we were unable to pull ourselves away until he left the parade deck. To our good luck, his platoon took a short cut back to the barracks via a break in the stands. As Nick passed by, I saw the slightest glance, eyes only, in our direction, then a miniscule rise, nearly undetectable, in the corner of his mouth.

"He knows we're here." I was jubilant.

"He's gonna make it," Dad said, all doubts erased over Nick's conversion from boy to Marine. "Yes, he sure is."

The next day was graduation, a ceremony full of formal traditions. The base band played and marched the length of the parade deck; the recruits marched in solemn formation; the senior drill instructors saluted each other with swords drawn. The base chaplain bestowed a blessing; the company commander presented individual awards; then it was time for each recruit to be given his Eagle, Globe, and Anchor pin, the symbol of the Marine, which identifies the bearer as having been accepted into the Corps. As the loudspeaker played Lee Greenwood's "I'm Proud to Be an American," I watched through the telephoto lens of my camera, snapping pictures, as Nick was handed his pin. He pinned it to his cap and returned to attention. When I pulled the camera away from my face, it was wet.

I am remembering all of this during my flight to Rochester. I want to say something to the new

Marine, some words of wisdom that would help him, inspire him, or perhaps soothe him in difficult times. I think about reminding him that he is now part of a brotherhood that reaches back to 1775, and to do his brothers—past, present, and future—proud. Or I could tell him to always watch for the Marine beside him, who just might be my son. Or maybe simply, "Be careful and good luck." I think back over the last eighteen months of my son's service, as I've watched him revel in achievements and wallow in disappointments as he's adjusted to Marine life. I wonder what words of advice would best serve this new warrior, this other mother's son, through the four years ahead.

We arrive in Rochester, and I exit the plane before the Marine and his family. I gather my courage to speak up, to tell him what I believe he needs to know. I see the family heading to baggage claim. More family members have come to greet him, and they cluster around the young Marine, a swarm of congratulations. It feels too private to interrupt, so I don't. But I send my message to him in my silent maternal language, the one that could make all the difference over the next four years: *Call your mother.*

Whenever he gets a chance, he should call his mother, even if there is nothing to say. For her to hear his voice, to hear his breathing and maybe his laughter is all she needs to stop her worrying, at least for that day. She let him go to a life he chose. It surely is not the one she would have chosen for him; never would she have put him in harm's way. Though he chose a path of honor and potential horror, she, too, will need strength to live with his choice. And although he may not realize her contribution to his well-being for years to come, the strength he draws from her will help see him through this. All he has to do to keep them both strong is to call. Those phone calls, as well as e-mails and letters, will fortify them through the days, weeks, and years ahead in his life as a United States Marine and in hers as a Marine mom.

Call your mother, new Marine. Even though you've told her not to worry, call to reassure her you're okay. Call so she can hear you breathing; maybe let a laugh escape so she knows that you are still her same boy. Call whenever you can, even if just for a moment, to remind you of the one who raised you and let you go. Call your mother to remind you that, no matter what happens, she loves you without end.

Call your mother.

—*Gretchen Stahlman*

Patriots Within All of Us

The young man in Army fatigues got on the plane for his first trip home in more than fifteen months. I was on the same plane headed to a business conference, with a side trip planned to visit close friends. He took the seat next to me and said he was coming in from Iraq, where he'd been stationed for well over a year. After that, he stayed mostly quiet. Any careful observer could tell by his wariness that he had experienced things over there that most Americans never will: acts of horror, acts of kindness, maybe even acts of faith. There was a certain dazed and confused look on his face that is seen only on veterans of foreign wars—the look that says, "I'm so thankful to be home on American soil, but I may never be the same again."

He looked to be in his early twenties and had blondish hair cut short and skin that was dry and sunburned. He sat still as the plane taxied and took off. Once in the air, I tried to engage him in conversation, but his short, though polite, responses made it clear he didn't want to talk. Or couldn't. He seemed bone tired. So I turned back to my book, and he leaned his head back and closed his eyes.

When the flight attendant stopped to take our drink orders, he opened his eyes and perked up. I figured he was excited to be able to have a cocktail now that he was stateside again. "Domestic beer," he said.

She chatted with him for a few minutes, and once she found out he was a soldier coming home for the first time, she whispered that the drinks were on the house. He seemed a little embarrassed but pleased at the same time.

She was true to her word, and every time his beer would start getting a bit low, she would magically appear with another. By the end of the trip, he must've had at least a six-pack, by my count. I was just hoping he wouldn't be driving anywhere near me when we got to Cleveland.

He must've been reading my mind, because he suddenly turned to me and said, "Don't worry; my folks will be driving me home, or my brother, or one of my friends. They should all be there to pick me up."

I smiled. "Sounds like a good family reunion."

"Any family reunion is a good one for me, that's for damn sure." He chuckled and then caught himself. Casting his eyes down, he said, "Oh, sorry about that, ma'am."

It took me a minute to realize he was apologizing for saying "damn."

"Oh, that's okay," I reassured him. "No problem."

Apparently that little exchange, and the beer, was the ice breaker. Now, he was ready to talk. He told me about the daily drill while he was in Iraq, how the troops never get any sleep and how sand gets in everything. He talked about his comrades, both the ones who had made it, so far, and those who hadn't. He seemed to feel a little bit guilty about coming home when so many others were still back there, fighting.

As the plane began its descent, he leaned his head back again and closed his eyes. The boy looked exhausted . . . and weary, war weary. I wondered what sort of family he came from and how much time he would get to spend with them before he shipped out again on his next assignment.

The plane bounced a few times on the final approach before settling smoothly on the runway. Then it turned left and stopped. While we were waiting for clearance to taxi over to our gate, the flight attendant came back on the intercom with her final instructions, along with an unusual request.

"If everyone could please quiet down for just a second." She paused as people reluctantly obliged. "We have a special guest onboard with us tonight," she said, looking directly to the back of the plane where we were sitting. "We have a young Army soldier who is returning home to his family after his first extended tour in Iraq. Out of our patriotic respect for him and for all the military does for us to keep freedom alive and to keep us safe, I respectfully request that you stay seated until this young man has a chance to deplane. He deserves to be the first one to see his family today."

There was a buzz of murmurs and shuffling as people swerved their heads around, trying to get a good look at who the attendant was talking about. Bashful and red-faced, with his head bowed, the young man stood up, collected his things, and quietly shuffled up the aisle toward the front of the plane.

As he passed each row of passengers, hands reached out to shake his or to pat him on the back, and several people handed him money. A pretty young girl even leaned over to kiss him on the cheek, which made his already red face turn almost crimson. A feeling of excitement and good will seemed to sweep up the aisle with him.

Sure enough, the soldier got off the plane and went straight into the arms of his loved ones. Tears flowed and relief flooded their faces at the sight of him, and as each of the other passengers passed by, they saluted him as if he were the commander in chief.

His family seemed genuinely surprised at all the attention he was getting. His mother was hugging him and wouldn't let go; his father was clearly as proud as any father could be; and his friends were socking him in the arm and ruffling his hair. He was home.

I will never forget the profound love and respect that we all felt toward that young soldier—and, I believe, toward our country. And it became very clear to me that day that no matter how each of us might feel about whatever war our country is engaged in, it really doesn't matter—as long as we pay our respects to the men and women fighting for our country. They deserve our respect, and they've earned it, whatever their role has been. They are patriots in the truest sense of the word. I also saw patriots in every one of those passengers that day. And it made me very proud to be an American.

—Susan Lynn Perry

Contributors

Tammera Ayers ("Miracle at Sea") is a licensed social worker with Senior Independence, the largest provider of retirement services in Ohio. She lives with her husband of nineteen years, three teenagers, and several animals on the St. Mary's River, where she writes, gardens, and participates in her local farmer's market.

Justin R. Ballard ("The Illusion"), a C-130 navigator, is stationed at Little Rock Air Force Base, Arkansas. Captain Ballard has traveled the world in both military and tourist aspects. He is husband to his best friend, Senéad, and a father to two beautiful daughters, Rachel and Addison, for whom he makes up stories and songs every day.

Janine Boldrin ("Sisterhood of the Traveling Pans") is a writer living in West Point, New York, with her husband and two sons. She wants to thank all of the Army wives who have knocked on her door over the years, carrying a hot meal or an invitation to dinner.

Rebecca Jayne Boswell ("Now I Know") lives in upstate New York. A teacher at Ellis College of New York Institute of Technology, she is also a writer, actor, singer, and life coach who delights in using her skills and talents to guide, educate, support, inspire, and motivate others.

Christy A. Caballero ("Respectful Warrior") is a freelance writer who grew up in an Air Force family. Her nationally recognized piece on the Vietnam War dogs received a Maxwell Award. After a childhood full of moving, she set down roots out between deer paths in Oregon. She laughs that she was born with eyes the same olive green as her dad's fatigues, not the blue she would've expected to inherit from him.

Ann Campanella ("Looking for Home") is the author of the poetry collection *What Flies Away*. After growing up in Jacksonville, Florida, the Panama Canal Zone, and

Morehead City, North Carolina, she has found a home in Huntersville, North Carolina, where she lives on a small horse farm with her husband and daughter.

Sarah Casey ("Memoir of an Army Girlfriend") is a full-time college student at Syracuse University. Originally from Plattsburgh, New York, she is a small-town girl with big dreams of one day running a newspaper or magazine of her own. She enjoys fishing, camping, and spending time with her family, friends, and military boyfriend.

Stephanie Cassatly ("Farewell at Gate Nine") is a writer, mother, and wife—not necessarily in that order. Having grown up an expatriate, she has traveled throughout Latin America, Europe, and Asia. She recently completed her masters in writing and is working on her memoir. She resides with her family in Jupiter, Florida.

Karen Gray Childress ("Day by Day") lives in Missouri and writes freelance, romance, and women's fiction. After years in the secretarial world, she now works at a grocery store, where she's inspired by the interesting stories of a variety of people. She loves to travel and to dabble in pastel art.

Ruth Douillette ("Alone in a Crowd" and "One Veteran's Story") is recently retired from teaching after thirty-five years. A writer, photographer, and associate editor of the *Internet Review of Books*, she is now busier than ever. Her essays have been published in *Christian Science Monitor*, *Chicken Soup* anthologies, and *Under Our Skin*, an anthology of breast cancer stories. Ruth is the yin to her former Marine husband's yang.

Liz Hoyt Eberle ("A [Nearly] Perfect Christmas") maintains her soul in Fredericksburg, Texas. She and her husband relish visits with their large blended family, country living, and Texas sunsets at their house on the hill. Between holiday and family celebrations, she writes family stories, works on novels, and explores history.

Ellen Fenner ("Fate and Forgiveness") lives in Odessa, Florida, where she left behind a career in sales to pursue a less conventional living as a mural artist, web designer, professional pet sitter, musician, and now writer. She is gathering her family lore with hope of someday writing a memoir about their fascinating lives. This is her first published story.

K. R. Fieser ("The Price of Freedom"), of western Pennsylvania, is passionate about art, singing, and family. With her children grown, she can no longer nose in on their essays, term papers, and reports and has subsequently resorted to writing her own stories to assuage her passion for the written word. A novel is in the works.

Linda Gammon ("Long Distance with My Brother") lives in Blue Springs, Missouri. When not spending time with her granddaughters, she substitute teaches, travels with her husband, works in her garden, writes personal essays and poetry, or makes coveted commemorative videos for family and friends.

Nichole A. Gifford ("The Next Fifth Date") has been pier-side with her husband in Virginia Beach, Virginia, for the past two-plus years. In addition to recording her thoughts and experiences as a Navy wife, she enjoys teaching, photography, and creating memories with her husband and their four furry family members.

Eileen Clemens Granfors ("On Time or Else"), a former Army brat and surfer girl, retired from teaching high school and joined the UCLA Writer's Program. She and her husband currently reside in Santa Clarita, California, and hope to move permanently to the peaceful beauty of their Ozarks lake home.

Lou Hamm ("Sentimental Journey") is a retired legal administrator living in Garrett, Indiana. During the fifteen years she has enjoyed writing nonfiction, she has had articles in a variety of publications and is the author of the book about a World War II experience, *Fondest Love—Yours Ian*. Married to her husband, Charley, for fifty-one years before his death in 1998, she has three children and one grandson.

Terri J. Haynes ("True Identity") keeps busy as a wife, mother of three, writer, and freelance graphic designer. She loves God and ministers to young adults alongside her husband. Her favorite things are books, shoes, and butterflies. She currently resides with her family in Fort Washington, Maryland.

Donna Lee Hines ("Stressed and Blessed") is an educator and retreat speaker. She enjoys sunrise over the Chesapeake Bay, playing guitar, and making waves in her boat for the dolphins to jump. Her husband is known to holler, "Girl, slow this boat down!" She responds with a grin. Her three grown sons grin, too.

Barbara J. Hollace ("Debt of Honor") is a freelance writer, speaker, and trainer. She and her Vietnam-veteran husband reside in Spokane Valley, Washington. Recently, she finished her first screenplay and is editing two novels. Writing is her passion. She says, "The greater the writing challenge, the greater my joy."

Melanie Saxer Johnston ("A Little Girl and a Big War") is a dog columnist and the author of the memoir, *What My Father Saw*. She gratefully shares her house in Northern California with her family as well as with Abby, a Bernese mountain dog, and Floyd E, a pug.

Mary Kuykendall-Weber ("In Sunshine and in Shadow") was born on a farm in West Virginia and now lives in Middle Grove, New York. After leaving her job with General Electric, she wrote a book on corporate greed, *The House that Jack Blew Down*, and a play, *Gold Collars*. A 2005 semifinalist in the 2005 Faulkner competition, she has received several other writing awards and has had one novella and more than forty stories published.

Mary Laufer ("The Backup Plan") is a freelance writer whose stories and poems have appeared in magazine and anthologies. A native of Western New York, she moved thirteen times while a Navy wife, attending five colleges and finally earning a degree in English. She lives in Forest Grove, Oregon, with her husband and daughter.

Allison L. Maher ("The World in My Hands") is a full-time farmer and part-time author. She published her first novel, *I, The Spy*, in 2006. She lives in rural Nova Scotia, Canada, with her husband and two children.

Lisa M. Maloney ("Wings to Fly, Arms to Hold Me") resides in Anchorage, Alaska, where she focuses on writing nonfiction and children's books. Thankful to have grown up as an Air Force child, now that she has put down roots, she spends a lot of time outside listening to trees and the wind.

Sascha Matuszak ("To Be the Son of a Soldier") is a road addict living in Chengdu, China, where he puts tall tales down on paper for his friends and enemies to read and laugh over. He grew up an Army brat, and the constant movement is locked in his veins. His next stop will be Portland, Oregon, where he will write modern ghost stories and go camping.

Rachel McClain ("The Spouses Club") is a mom who currently lives and suns in Los Angeles but loves everywhere the military sends her. Married to an Air Force officer, Rachel is a former Air Force officer herself who left the service to raise their son and to pursue writing. She is published in several online magazines and is finishing her first young-adult novel.

Paula Munier ("Home Is Not a Place for Me") was born at Fort Sill, Oklahoma, and has lived in more than forty houses/ apartments/quarters in thirty-four towns/cities/posts scattered across more than a dozen states/countries/bases in Europe and the Continental United States. A veteran writer and editor, she lives on the South Shore in Massachusetts. If she's still there by the time you hold this book in your hands, it will be the longest she's ever lived anywhere in her life.

Denise Neumann ("Engine Run") is an Air Force spouse who, after six moves in seven years, has decided to give up unpacking and follow her bliss in writing. She loves being a wife and the mother of two amazing young children as well as volunteering with the Deployment and Mobilization side of the Air Force Family Center.

Susan Lynn Perry ("Patriots Within All of Us") is a freelance writer of numerous articles, short stories, novels, and nonfiction books. In her newest book, *Mother Cub*, she shares the challenges and joys of helping her son emerge from autism. She currently resides in Texas, where she continues to inspire other parents every day.

Lisa A. Phillips ("The Fabric of a Seasoned Navy Wife") is a retired Navy wife who resides with her husband and her two children in Arlington, Washington. She oversees the financial accounting of their family business, leads a women's ministry, and pursues writing opportunities as time permits.

David W. Powers, Th.D., ("A Leatherneck Legacy") is a tireless entrepreneur who has started and operated a number of profitable businesses, including a specialty remodeling firm in Myrtle Beach, South Carolina. Often called "the most educated man in construction," he has six college degrees, including a doctorate. He is the author of eight books and more than 250 articles.

Linda M. Powers ("When Dad Leaves for War: Connor's Story") is the proud mom of a son, Jody, presently serving in Iraq, as well as a daughter, Ashley, and her husband, Matt. A certified pharmacy technician, she lives in Westfield, Massachusetts.

Amy Bladow Rivard ("Do What You Have to Do") recently made yet another military move to Fort Carson, Colorado. She loves to paint and write, and plans to write and illustrate children's books after she unpacks. A full-time mother and Army wife, she somehow found time to write a novel for her daughters that she hopes will find a publisher.

S. Ann Robinson ("You *Are* the Mom") worked for four decades as an instructor, business manager, seminar leader, staff writer, wife, and mother. She now lives in northern Virginia, where she teaches at the local community college, attends American Sign Language classes, writes for regional publications, and enjoys nurturing her granddaughter, Victoria.

Sallie A. Rodman ("Her Heart Is Red, White, and Blue") is an award-winning author whose work has appeared in numerous *Chicken Soup* anthologies, various magazines, and the *Orange County Register*. She lives with her husband Paul and Inky the cat in Los Alamitos, California.

Employed as the director of trade at a local port, she enjoys writing and doing mixed-media art.

Tammy Ruggles ("Hero in the House") writes articles, children's stories, and screenplays. Her first book, *Peace*, was published in 2005 by Clear Light Books. She lives in Maysville, Kentucky.

Edie Barton Scher ("A Sailor's Return") is a writer whose work appears in national publications, including the first *Cup of Comfort*® anthology. Her children, grandchildren, family, and good friend, Max, are constant sources of inspiration. She currently teaches English at the Academy for Allied Health Sciences in Scotch Plains, New Jersey, where her students bring joy to each day.

Terence M. Shumaker ("Cry for Happy"), his wife, Lonnie, and their Scottish terrier share twenty-seven acres with the trees and wildlife along the Old Oregon Trail, east of Oregon City, Oregon. A retired college instructor, he now updates his textbooks, works on a novel, and flies above the green hills of Oregon whenever he can.

Verna L. Simms ("Not Navy Knots") is a freelance writer and a retired librarian. Her late husband, Howard, served as a CB in the Navy during World War II. The couple was married for sixty-six years, during which they raised two daughters and shared several grandchildren.

Gretchen Stahlman ("Advice for a New Marine") is a technical writer living in upstate New York. She is proud of her son's service and his tours in Iraq but is very relieved to have him out of harm's way. She says, "I could write a manual on how to worry during deployment."

Melinda Fay Stanley ("Gung Ho") is an Indiana Hoosier working in resource development. She has four adult children and two grandbabies. She has written a contemporary romantic suspense novel and is plotting her second novel, a paranormal romantic fantasy.

Travis B. Tougaw ("Unspoken") has served as a public affairs officer and English instructor in the U.S. Air Force. He currently works in the education department of a health-care system in Texas, where he lives with his wife and son in San Antonio.

Lauren M. Turner ("For Every Tear, a Smile") is a student at University of Maryland. She and her husband, Rich, are originally from the Washington, D.C., area. She enjoys spending time with the couple's dogs and is extremely dedicated to her family, who are an inspiration to her.

Donna Duly Volkenannt ("Welcome Home") lives in Missouri with her husband, Walter, and their grandchildren, Cari and Michael, who fill her heart with joy. When not reading, writing, or carpooling, she can be found watching Michael play baseball, soccer, or basketball and watching Cari at soccer, volleyball, or Irish dancing.

Julie A. Whan ("Such Purpose that Drives Them") lives in Erie, Pennsylvania, and is a purchasing manager for a glass company. The author of several published stories, she recently obtained a B.A. in English and is working on her first novel.

Katie Wigington ("Please Tie Your Shoes") lives in Charlotte, North Carolina, with her three dogs, Smokie, Noodlehead, and Toshi. She is a successful real estate broker and a loving mother to her son, Nick, and his wife, Galina. In addition to writing her monthly *Real Estate Gazette*, she pens short stories and articles.